What I **Know** to Be True

Six Simple Words to Set You Free

LISA JACOBY & CAROLINE J TEMPLE

BALBOA.
PRESS
A DIVISION OF HAY HOUSE

Balboa Press books may be ordered through booksellers or by contacting:
Balboa Press
A Division of Hay House
1663 Liberty Drive
Bloomington, IN 47403
www.balboapress.com
1-(877) 407-4847

Because of the dynamic nature of the Internet, any web addresses or links contained in this book may have changed since publication and may no longer be valid. The views expressed in this work are solely those of the author and do not necessarily reflect the views of the publisher, and the publisher hereby disclaims any responsibility for them.

The author of this book does not dispense medical advice or prescribe the use of any technique as a form of treatment for physical, emotional, or medical problems without the advice of a physician, either directly or indirectly. The intent of the author is only to offer information of a general nature to help you in your quest for emotional and spiritual well-being. In the event you use any of the information in this book for yourself, which is your constitutional right, the author and the publisher assume no responsibility for your actions.

Cover design by Kathleen Griswold.
Icon art by Anna Linley.
Poem "The Seed" © Cindy Marcus 2011.

ISBN: 978-1-4525-4225-6 (e)
ISBN: 978-1-4525-4226-3 (sc)
ISBN: 978-1-4525-4227-0 (hc)

Library of Congress Control Number: 2011919810

Printed in the United States of America

Balboa Press rev. date: 02/10/2012

To John, Max & Declan, who have always given
me the space to find my own Truth.
To Joy & Larry, who were the first to teach me
to find my own Truth.
To Laurie, who has been as much of a mirror for me
as she says I have been for her.
To Caroline, the perfect partner for this work
and who teaches me every day.

To Damian, who has shown unwavering belief in me
and in this book.
To David, Ian and Chris, who always have the courage
to follow their own hearts.
To my sister, Brigid, with thanks for a lifetime
of love and support.
To Lisa, who has taught me so much about what it means
to live in my own Truth.

To our Miss A
Antoinette Martignoni, our role model for living
her own Truth even when she didn't know it!

What I *Know* to Be True

To See the Truth is
Informative;
*To Know the Truth is
Transformative.*

Acknowledgements

We wish to express heartfelt appreciation to our friends and families, whose assistance and suggestions were so valuable, and whose encouragement was immeasurable. To our Friends & Sisters, you know who you are, for being there for us and for believing in this work. We are particularly grateful to Linda Sivertsen for exceptional insights and editing; Damian Nance, for an ever calming presence and focused line editing; Anna Linley, for creating brilliantly intuitive artwork; Cindy Marcus, for conjuring up the perfect poem to complement our work; Ian Temple, for his willingness to give up a Sunday in order to capture the perfect audio recording; Patricia Spadaro, Nigel Yorwerth, and Maree Macpherson, for their initial guidance and pointing us in the right direction.

Special love and appreciation to our early Supporters & Encouragers, who saw the potential from the outset: Krissy Dorn, Denise Romano, Trudy & Bob Griswold, Brigid Legge, Raffaello Di Meglio, Lizanne Megrue, Emily Morrison, Jennifer Martin, Terry Wright, and Kathy Caprino. To our friend in spirit, Lily Siegel, who helped open the gateway for us to discover the true depth of this practice.

To all of you who embraced practicing *What I **Know** to Be True* as we perfected it, including Kay Griswold, Laurie Cameron, Bob Bronzo, Lisa Cimino, and all of our workshop participants; you have helped us more than you know.

"What I *Know*
to Be True"
confirms and nourishes your
inner power, teaching you
to embrace yourself without
requiring the approval,
blessing or agreement of
another.

Contents

Preface

What if you could retain your sense of self, your sense of equilibrium, even in the face of life's most difficult and painful lessons? What if you could let go of what others think about you, your actions, and your choices, thereby reclaiming your personal power? Instead of being consumed by your problems and emotions, what if you could respond to them with grace and ease? What if you could connect to your deepest wisdom to feel safe and secure, regardless of circumstance? Imagine if you could do all that and still retain an open heart!

The truth is that you can! You have all the resources you need right inside yourself; you just have to learn how to tap into them.

The words "What I *Know* to Be True" offer freedom from the perceived chaos, unhappiness and lack of control in your life, to a sense of internal balance and harmony, whatever storm is raging on the surface.

That's a bold statement, for sure. How can six simple words offer such a big promise? We wouldn't have believed it either, if we hadn't experienced the remarkable benefits firsthand.

What I **Know** *to Be True* is a book, a practice, a way of life. It is the key for you to connect to the Truth—or knowing—that resides deep within each of you and acts as your personal GPS for how to live with greater ease. **You will learn to know your Truth, trust that you can depend on it, and use it as a guide to live by.**

You are the gateway, What I *Know* to Be True is the key.

Know your Truth

Trust your Truth

Live your Truth

You are the Gateway
What I Know to Be True
is the Key

Our Stories

Lisa

I have, for a long time, considered myself to be well-developed spiritually. From a young age, I was interested in personal growth, development, and all things unexplained. I had read a tremendous range of books on subjects from becoming clutter-free to life-after-death. I'd studied different spiritual perspectives from Native American to Buddhist, attended workshops and seminars, from Werner Erhard's EST in the 1970's to Abraham-Hicks' more recent *The Art of Allowing*.. With all that "enlightenment" I felt I had become a fairly centered, clear-eyed individual who could handle most of life's challenges with grace and ease.

And so it was with great surprise that I found myself responding to a stressful situation with a significant lack of grace. In the process of dissolving a business partnership, my partners had a decidedly different perspective than I about how to share in the sale proceeds. After much (and sometimes heated) dialogue back and forth it became apparent that there was heightened negative emotion on all sides attached to our perspectives.

I was angry that my partners did not agree with me. I felt my proposal was more than fair. How could we be so far off in our perspectives? I found myself stewing about the perceived unfairness, thoughts and emotions swirling continuously in my head. The cloud of the situation followed my every move, affecting all of my activities. I was trapped in the pain of the situation.

As time passed, I realized I felt wounded, as if my partners failed to value any of the contributions I had made in creating our successful business. I believed that their suggested remuneration diminished my efforts. (They, of course, felt the same diminishment from my offer.)

When I realized the truth of my "wounding" reaction I was able to gain more perspective and approach the disagreement more objectively. I did still feel, however, that I needed to honor myself and be honest about how I felt. I offered a compromised solution. The compromise was also rejected and I faced yet another wounding.

I was stuck. Their combined vote in the partnership outweighed mine; there was no recourse. How was I to live with this? Not only was I feeling wounded but friendships were at stake. Clearly this was a core issue for me. What had happened in my childhood that allowed for this reaction? Was it from another lifetime, perhaps? An unresolved karmic issue? Whatever the source, the pain that surfaced was real and breathtaking in its effect. When I was able to focus on the feelings that arose, my list read like this:

"I feel less than, small, unworthy, undeserving, dumb, incapable, ineffective."

The tears flowed.

I felt just like the little girl who used to hide under the coffee table when visitors arrived. So terribly shy, I sometimes wanted to disappear from the world. I'm not sure what I was afraid people would see, I only knew that perceived strangers, even my own grandparents, imposed pain just by requiring my interaction. Making myself smaller allowed me to escape interactions and minimize my pain, or so I thought.

Now it appeared that my child-self was now in charge. But why?

Where was the enlightened perspective I needed at this moment in time? Where were the universal lessons I thought I understood and was trying to live my life by? I started saying daily affirmations and prayers to help heal my issues of self-worth. I knew that if I didn't address this, my issues would continue to surface.

Meditating one morning, I flashed on the most recent communication from my partners, which outlined the reasons they felt I was not entitled to a greater share of the proceeds. The pain in my gut raged, and I thought, "How can I clear this for myself? How can I heal this?"

And then I heard myself say to myself:

I feel wounded by another who does not value my contribution, **however,**

+ *What I **Know** to Be True* is that I *have* made a significant contribution.

+ *What I **Know** to Be True* is that my contribution may not be reflected monetarily.

+ *What I **Know** to Be True* is that my participation created good will and generated revenue.

+ *What I **Know** to Be True* is that I recognize my contribution, even if others do not, and that is enough.

+ *What I **Know** to Be True* is that I can hear and understand my partners even if I have a different perspective.

+ *What I **Know** to Be True* is that I am a whole and healthy individual.

- *What I **Know** to Be True* is that I have tremendous gifts.

- *What I **Know** to Be True* is that I will use my tremendous gifts for other projects.

- *What I **Know** to Be True* is that by holding onto this wound I will not be able to release it and move forward.

- *What I **Know** to Be True* is that this realization does not minimize the truth of my emotional response to the situation.

- *What I **Know** to Be True* is that this realization allows me to remember my core truth, which is the essence of my being and all that really matters.

Coming out of that meditation, I felt a huge physical change, as if from every cell of my being.

The words and practice of what would become known as *"What I **Know** to Be True"* had connected me with non-physical Source in a direct and powerful way, with clarity and purity that acted like a brilliant white light. It brought me back to my knowing, *my higher Truth*. This was Truth beyond doubt, Truth without judgment, Truth that could not be swayed. I felt weightless and liberated, filled with the lightness of being and the lightness of spirit. By choosing to get quiet and meditate I had touched on something incredibly simple, yet deeply powerful at the same time.

Feeling like I could take flight, vibrating with joy and excitement, I anticipated all the good things to come. There was no longer room for resentment or hurt. I didn't know what to do; the energy was flowing so profoundly. It was hard to remember a time when I'd felt so exalted, so radiant, or so open to the possibilities.

I recognized that the *What I **Know** to Be True* statements coming to me were Truth I was *remembering* from the *Me* that I'd disconnected from in my pain. The *Me* that is the conscious connection to Source. They were the gateway that took me beyond the words we've been taught to say or believe, to the Truth I could *feel*.

The next thought I had was that I needed to share this with others. I thought of my friend Caroline, a holistic psychotherapist, with whom I'd recently shared a touching synchronistic moment. The next morning Caroline and I were scheduled to have breakfast and I couldn't wait to share my new-found practice.

I pulled out the printed pages I'd written about my A-ha moment along with additional examples. She read the first one and began to cry. She read another one and felt completely overwhelmed, explaining that I'd captured an issue that spoke to the core of something that had recently surfaced for her, an issue she'd been struggling with for some time.

From there, our discussions led naturally and almost instantly to the creation of this simple, yet powerful practice. We knew our collaboration would continue to help us in our own journeys of growth, and at the same time benefit others. But it took another two years of living with and using the practice of *What I **Know** to Be True* to truly understand how to best share the profound changes it afforded.

Caroline

Unlike Lisa, I had always struggled with meditation, having fallen prey to the myths of "I should be able to empty my mind completely" or it being something that "I can't do." Busy looking outside myself for the answers, I seldom had enough patience to sit quietly with myself long enough for any wisdom to show up! I attended workshops and read books, visited psychics and studied new spiritual tools, adding one at a time to my toolbox and building on the excitement of previous discoveries. Still, I yearned for the sense of peace that others seemed to have, but which I struggled to find. Although I was aware of an overall uneasiness, coupled with a continual sense of anxiety and stress, up until that day at the diner with Lisa, I had been doing a decent job of ignoring the signals.

That's when all the shame I'd been sitting on became undeniable.

It had been a year since I'd made the very difficult decision to end my marriage and move out of our dream house on the water. I'd desperately hurt and angered both my husband and my children. I lost friends. I felt judged by others and further judged myself, internalizing that judgment as shame. "I must be a bad person," I thought. I felt afraid of what others would think. Blaming myself harshly, I isolated and hid from others, becoming more and more miserable the more I alienated myself. I tried to reconcile my actions and find peace in the paradox of knowing that I had followed my own truth to get here, but the cloak of shame enveloped me. I wanted the feelings to go away; I wanted to fix the problem. I focused on helping others instead of myself, but the more I focused on others, the more the uncomfortable feelings appeared in front of me, as if to say "here I am again." In fact, the more determined I was to escape or justify the truth of my feelings, the heavier and more painful they became. Inevitably, the day came when I hit bottom emotionally, looked myself in the mirror and stepped onto the long hard road of healing.

It was shortly thereafter that Lisa introduced me to *What I Know to Be True*. The relief I felt in that moment was palpable. I could FEEL the shift immediately. There was actually a way to support the inner truth that I had been hanging onto for dear life, (the one telling me that I was not a bad person), while at the same time take responsibility for my actions and acknowledge the hurt I had caused others without drowning in it any longer.

I was ashamed of my behavior, **however…**

+ *What I **Know** to Be True* is that I am only human and as such I will inevitably struggle with difficult decisions.

+ *What I **Know** to Be True* is that my mistakes don't make me a bad person.

+ *What I **Know** to Be True* is that facing my truth with honesty and integrity will set me free from shame.

+ *What I **Know** to Be True* is that I can support myself better if I stop judging myself so harshly.

+ *What I **Know** to Be True* is that I am here to learn and this experience holds a wealth of teaching, if I choose to listen to my inner wisdom.

+ *What I **Know** to Be True* is that I deserve to be happy and fulfilled.

+ *What I **Know** to Be True* is that I can apologize to the people I hurt by telling them the truth.

+ *What I **Know** to Be True* is that by holding onto this shame and continuing to hide, I will forestall my healing and growth.

+ *What I **Know** to Be True* is that if I really tap into my Truth, I will be guided and fully supported on my journey.

+ *What I **Know** to Be True* is that I am not alone.

The practice of *What I **Know** to Be True* reminded me that, even though I was feeling tremendously sad and guilty about some of my choices, I was not a bad person. Of course, there was more internal work to be done. I continued to explore and feel my way through it, with the help of therapy and spiritual reflection, readings, workshops and the love of my friends and family. Being honest with myself, and Lisa, and using the words *What I **Know** to Be True*, immediately shifted my internal battle. It was as if both voices could put down their weapons, call a truce and move forward. That was the moment I began to see beyond the shame. I began to forgive myself for my many mistakes and look to the future as a stronger, wiser person, determined to learn from my experiences and live more fully in Truth.

The decision to partner with Lisa on writing this book was an easy one for me. I discovered that not only did *What I **Know** to Be True* have deep resonance for me personally, it was also a perfect complement to the work I was already doing as I sought to help my therapy clients find relief from the intensity of difficult feelings and experiences. In teaching others to tap into their own truth through the practice of *What I **Know** to Be True*, I have found a more centered, calmer place in the here and now, for both myself and those I seek to help. I have also discovered that this concept has the power to help access a connection to something bigger, something more meaningful and universal. My life is enriched beyond belief as a result of using this simple, powerful tool.

After two years of collaborating with Lisa, I have learned to use *What I **Know** to Be True* on many different levels. It has helped me get in touch with my true self, the one I had kept hidden behind the encumbrance of unworthiness and the barrage of negative mental chatter. The window opened up to allow me to see and be seen with honesty and vulnerability. *What I **Know** to Be True* helped me to deepen my journey of seeking my Truth and finding out who I really am. I know it will do the same for you.

What began as a gift we used to ease the pain of emotional situations has evolved into an on-going journey of self-discovery and freedom. You will have different burdens, challenges, and experiences to address in your own life. And, whatever they may be, however large or small, the practice of *What I Know to Be True* will help you navigate rough waters towards a more centered, peaceful and conscious you.

The Way In

~~~

> *Saying the words What I **Know** to Be True acts as a cue, a prompt that immediately shifts you to your center. The words short-circuit what the mind is telling you, allowing you to open your heart and find peace, regardless of what is going on around you.*

*What I **Know** to Be True* is a book, a phrase, a practice, a way of life. These six simple words that showed up like a gift will help you in many ways. They will:

+ transform your life on a daily basis and provide relief from stress

+ teach you how to love yourself while judging yourself (and others) less

+ offer relief from the intensity of difficult feelings and experiences

+ reduce reactivity in emotionally charged situations

- help you to find the "pause" required to detach from controlling emotions

- support and connect you with yourself and others even when you are feeling unhappy, misunderstood or alone

- help diffuse conflict

- provide an affirmation and reminder to center yourself in every day moments of your life

- create a meditation to reconnect with your higher self, with Source, with universal energy

- teach you how to connect with your true self

What I **Know** *to Be True* is a practice that helps you discover *your* Truth. What do we mean? We're referring to the Truth that comes from your higher self, the place of all-knowing Source. It is the Truth that resonates with the best expression of yourself, and confidently aligns you with a feeling of clarity and purity. It connects you with the divine in you, full of love and grace, and always there for you. It invites you to experience a return to Source, teaches you how to find peace when there appears to be none, and how to find connection when you feel alone and afraid. It will bring your attention to the wisdom of your soul, something bigger than you that is only known and experienced inside of you.

Truth comes with ease. It cannot be learned or forced. It needs to be experienced. We are wiser than our brains, deeper than our thoughts. Truth is felt differently for each of us. Truth is not found in someone else's words. It is not found in intellect or in the reading of yet another spiritual book, including this one. It is not found by looking to another's version of truth or through external validation. It is found in the core of each of us. It is found in "being" in stillness, not in "doing" or taking on more. Give yourself a break. Pause and exhale. Step back from the myriad of thoughts, and see how a bird's eye view changes your perception. Inner peace is found in Truth–your Truth. Learn to trust yourself through this practice.

In the pages that follow we offer guidelines for the practice of *What You **Know** to Be True*. You can open this book at any page and find a new teaching to use and reflect upon, new ways to consider your Truth, or simply a gentle reminder to go within. We offer suggestions for ways you can use the practice, such as a soothing tool, an affirmation upon waking, or as a deeply profound meditation in times of emotional crisis. Experiential examples are provided for you throughout.

And finally, we give you **Truisms**–or universal truths–that stimulate you to observe your thoughts and emotions and help you shift to a more powerful and conscious way of living when you're feeling at all disempowered.

For example:

+ *What I **Know** to Be True* is that my emotions do not define my reality.

+ *What I **Know** to Be True* is that I am never truly alone.

+ *What I **Know** to Be True* is that all is well.

We invite you to read what we share with an open mind and more importantly, with an open heart. Say the *What I **Know** to Be True* statements aloud and feel what resonates with *you*. Dip into the *Truisms*. Come back to them after letting the words marinate within you for a day, a week, a month. Don't take our word for it; don't accept them as your *Truth* unless you *feel* them as *Truth*.

They may not be *your Truth*, yet they may be a catalyst for you to find your own *Truth*. Explore your own *Truth* through *feeling*. Get comfortable *feeling* your own *Truth*. Express your own *Truth* out loud. Capture your own *Truth* in writing. Decide to live your own *Truth* and allow others to live theirs. Live your life in the only way that truly matters, from a place of *your own Truth*.

Why We Need
What I Know to Be True

～～～ ～～～

And several other key thoughts before getting started...

The Power of Setting an Intention

We can help minimize the power loss caused by rushing through life on auto-pilot by regularly setting our intention to live in Truth and connection. If we choose to, we can call in our guides (such as a higher power or angels) to support ourselves. Of course, it is easier to connect to ourselves while away on vacation or on retreat, but we inevitably fall back into a lack of awareness once back in our daily routine. Adopting *What I Know to Be True* into our language, our routine and our daily life, creates a new reality based in Truth, not illusion. ***What I Know to Be True* is that *setting an intention* is the way to begin this shift.**

Attend to your Suffering

We are a complex tangle of experiences, beliefs and emotions, some of which are responsive to present situations, some are reflexes learned in childhood, and many are of unidentifiable origin. Whatever the source of the emotional reaction, when the emotional mind becomes too powerful, the negative ego steps in and the relief found in Truth is overshadowed. If the emotional response controls you, it will cause you to act from an unhealthy place of ego, messing with your perspective, clarity and decision-making ability, not to mention your reactions of blame and shame. The defensive behavior that results from taking things personally only serves to create more pain and suffering, leading you even further from your Truth.

Practicing *What I **Know** to Be True* will help you begin to regulate such controlling emotions, allowing you to separate from the emotional ego identity and begin the process of healing through connection with your Truth. Stepping outside yourself to observe the emotion, without judgment, provides the perspective from which you are able to see that, while the emotion is real, it is not *who* you are.

By learning to pause, breathe, and look at yourself through your observing eye, you can stop the runaway train of your negative thoughts and choose instead to reconnect with your Truth. Just as a baby begins to realize that she/he is separate from her/his mother, you realize that you are separate from your thoughts. You are no more connected to them than you are any longer in the same body as your mother. Learning to quiet the ego with consistent use of this practice will build on itself, eventually causing a fundamental shift away from ego (where fear and disconnection, doubt and pain live) to your own connected Truth (where you feel a sense of belonging and deep trust of what is happening, even if it is difficult or painful.) The pain brings a message to your body that it is time to pay attention.

A wound left untended will not heal—it needs your attention in order to transform. It requires more than just acceptance. The practice of *What I Know to Be True* will help you witness and attend to your suffering. *What I Know to Be True* connects you to your wise compassionate self who can sit with your body, sit with your feelings, sit with your suffering. Connection with your Truth is a slow building of a new relationship with your self, free from the beliefs you have internalized and the judgments you have inevitably formed. It cannot be forced. It is gradual and gentle, rooted in kindness and compassion. It is where you find true peace and self-acceptance; a place of deep connection within yourself. You will know it when you meet it again. **What I Know to Be True helps us remember what we already know.**

Detach from the Energies and Emotions of Others

Whether or not we are aware of it, we are constantly taking on the energies and emotions of others, especially those of family and friends. We often unconsciously absorb negativity and toxic energy, not only on a personal level, but also from reading or hearing about national and global events. This upsets our internal alignment, changes our daily outlook and affects our ability to stay connected to our Truth.

It is imperative to become conscious of the effect of picking up unwanted emotions (for example, fear), as well as observing when others are tapping into our energy or asking us to take on their problems. Once we are aware this is happening, we can gently detach with compassion, soothe our own sensitivities, stay protected yet open, and ultimately not be impacted by the emotional energy of those around us. **What I Know to Be True is that our responsibility lies in staying grounded and centered in our own Truth.**

Taming your Ego

One of the essential steps in connecting with yourself in Truth is to be able to differentiate between what looks like truth (ego) and the Truth that is from your soul. So what is ego? It is a construct of our own mind; it doesn't really exist. We cannot point to our body and locate our ego. It is better known as the familiar voice in our head that is often negative, judgmental and destructive. The one that keeps us feeling less than, separate from, and unworthy. The one that has to be "right." It tricks us into believing that it is truth when in reality it may house pain, isolation, loneliness, separateness—from ourselves and others—that leads to depression, anxiety and poor life choices. A healthy ego is important, encouraging us to excel, but the dark side of the ego needs to be quieted so it doesn't become too all-consuming. **What I Know to Be True allows us to quiet the ego, rather than be at its mercy.**

Heart versus Head

The perception of a "heart-centered" person is not often a complimentary one; heart wisdom is discounted in this age of reason. In truth, we cannot choose to be *either* heart centered *or* logical (although this imbalance does occur). We need both heart *and* head. Heart wisdom is infinitely wise and solidly grounded in Truth. When we come first from the heart, we come from love, compassion, gentleness, knowing and Truth.

However, as children, we tend to be labeled as "too sensitive," or "overly emotional" when we show pain or are honest with our feelings. If this is the case, we grow up believing this sensitivity to be a "bad" thing; we doubt ourselves and end up living in the deep chasm between who we really are and who we've been told we should be. Be aware of the danger of "should" thinking; it is a critical, condemning voice that brings doubt to our wisdom.

The outside voices have the potential to quiet our wise hearts and invade our knowing.

Re-integration requires honoring the wisdom of our hearts, supporting our true selves by wisely using our intellect and logic. The truth is that we are best served by finding a balance that both honors heart-wisdom and head-wisdom, with heart leading the way. **What I Know to Be True helps us reconnect with our hearts.**

What it means to be Heart-Centered versus Emotionally Centered

It is important to understand the difference between being heart-centered and emotionally-centered. We know that we cannot be driven by our emotions, for this means that we are allowing our emotions to be in the driver's seat with us in the passenger seat, blindfolded. We feel out of control and reactive. To be heart-centered, on the other hand, feels quite different because it's centered, grounded and fully connected to Source. It is mature and wise, fully and quietly in charge, driven by neither emotion nor intellect, but by the Truth known only to self. Heart is home to Truth. It is essential for the good of humanity that we nourish the kind of love that can remain steady, even in the face of painful and blustering winds. **What I Know to Be True enables us to have the kind of compassion and empathy we need for others and the world, without being rocked by events going on in and around us.**

Searching for Security

We spend much of our lives searching for security. Whether we believe we weren't nurtured enough as a child or we experienced real physical or emotional trauma at an early age, most of us retain some underlying sense of insecurity about who we are in the world, our physical safety, and our financial well-being. Insecurity manifests in worrying about whether we are liked, and attaches itself to fear-based "what if…" thinking. It gives us a fundamental lack of trust in ourselves and the universe. We spend countless hours needlessly worrying about a secure future, seeking a certainty that we believe will make us feel safer, physically and emotionally. We often make decisions, such as choosing a mate, based on the need for feeling secure. In fact, many major decisions involving career, money, lifestyle and relationships are made out of our need for security (as well as our perceived place in the world).

In reality, security is an illusion. Our sense of security can only be derived from within, trusting in ourselves and the universe. In the here and now. *What I Know to Be True* **helps us to connect with this ultimate source of security.**

Giving up Control

The reward of "accepting" and "letting go" is a feeling of relief and ease, even if it initially feels quite the opposite. We must first give up the fight (often subconscious) against what appears to be happening. Pushing back against it is nothing but an energy drain and does not serve us in any way. The process of letting go begins with allowing, moving towards acceptance and eventually disempowering the negative energy of whatever situation in which we find ourselves, so that we can fully let go of our attachment to it. Sadness or hurt may remain but they do not paralyze us if we are accepting. There are some things in life that we just cannot change. There are some things in life for which we are not responsible. However, we can let go of the struggle by accepting and choosing to align with a more productive channel for our energies. **The paradox is that striving for control actually strips us of our power.** *What I Know to Be True* **helps us to give up the struggle and let go.**

Learning to Trust

If trust is the opposite of control, and control is a form of distraction from our Truth, then it speaks to reason that trust is an important element of a relationship with our all-knowing Truth. Not only is it difficult for us to trust others, especially when we have been hurt, but the layers of self-doubt, criticism, disappointment, and abandonment that have built up throughout our lifetimes makes it even harder for us to trust ourselves.

Trusting ourselves and others involves risk–the risk to let go of control, the risk to build safety within ourselves and attend to our own needs. It may mean facing our greatest fears, challenging ourselves to believe even when we don't, being vulnerable in the world. When we were a small child we innately trusted that our needs would be met. Then at some point in our lives, the foundation of trust that we were born with was undermined and worn away, often without intent from those who loved us, until we locked away that trusting, vulnerable self and threw away the key.

What I Know to Be True will help us face our vulnerable self and know that we can take care of ourselves, whatever the circumstance. The more we nourish our own connection with Truth, the more we can trust our ability to reach for a feeling of connection, ease, joy and lightness of being, even when we are afraid. It is a cycle that is repeated again and again–feeling a lack of trust, taking the risk, building trust–a cycle that builds on itself as we deepen our connection with source.

Staying in the present helps us to *feel* more in control, and therefore to feel a greater sense of trust, as does letting go of the outcome of a situation or not projecting onto others or looking too far into the future. Having *What I Know to Be True* at our fingertips allows us to take the risk to trust that all is–and will be–well. ***What I Know to Be True* is that ultimately we can Trust ourselves and our deep connection to Truth.**

I AM Good Enough

At the core of almost every emotional challenge are issues of self-worth, and concern about what others think of us. Self-esteem really means "the regard in which I hold myself." Yet it is so influenced by others that perhaps we should name it "others esteem." Healthy self-esteem is evident in one who trusts, and is guided by, his or her own voice, rather than the words or opinions of others. The regard in which we hold ourselves is therefore self-inflicted, within our influence to support and change. Simple, but not easy.

We tend to pay more heed to the negative messages we're given as we try to establish our own identity than we do to the positive mirrors all around us and from within our souls. This is particularly true if we have had critical parents or been in relationships where we are put down or demeaned. We start to believe those negative mirrors as Truth, other people's truth for us, and we even join in the chorus of negativity and judgment, thereby perpetuating the cycle of believing we're not good enough. Our own perfection becomes buried under the barrage of right-wrong, good-bad, black-white thoughts, mostly self-induced.

We must learn to shift our thinking away from these absolutes and stand, instead, in our own Truth—which is neither "good" nor "bad," "right" nor "wrong." Our self-regard will change when we deeply love and accept ourselves just the way we are. This is the starting place from which to make adjustments to our path, based on telling ourselves the Truth lovingly and without judgment. It is the beginning of a return to Source. It will require unpacking the myriad of old messages and internalized beliefs, but it starts with a decision to look at ourselves through a new lens, a lens of Truth, reflecting everything just as it is. *What I **Know** to Be True* will help you to recognize that self-esteem begins by planting the seed of self-acceptance and positive self-regard. ***What I Know to Be True*** connects us with the Source that *always* regards us in highest esteem, regardless of circumstance or behavior.

Where do I Belong?

From the moment we learn that we are separate beings from our mothers, we are encouraged to foster our separateness and independence from each other. The paradox begins as we struggle with being both separate and connected. The messages we learn are mixed, ranging from expectations to fit in, often put upon us by well-meaning authority figures, to being encouraged to grow, mature and "separate" from our families. To varying degrees, we have all been raised by a set of confusing rules and expectations, a push-pull of cries of "belong" and "be separate." We fear our separateness, our show of being different, even as we seek it. At some point, we start asking ourselves "Where do I fit in?" or "Who am I?" thoughts often accompanied by judgment and a sense of disconnect, both from the way we are "supposed to be" and from our true selves.

Metaphorically speaking, we humans cut the umbilical cord to the connectedness and oneness of all universal energies. We dislike not feeling as if we belong, as much as we fear too much connection. **What I Know to Be True helps us to remember both our connectedness and our uniqueness. It helps us to celebrate our sense of belonging as one small and unique piece of a gigantic universal puzzle, flawless in its creation.**

Finding Meaning and Purpose in our Lives

When we move towards connection with our own Truth, that which is divine and universal, we find expansive meaning and purpose in our lives. The feeling of connection is a key ingredient to feeling good about ourselves. It *feels* right. It doesn't mean there is no more pain or suffering; on the contrary. Releasing ourselves from the vice-like grip of pain begins with a compassionate witnessing of that pain. Developing a relationship with our own Truth strips down all the ineffectual deception we have learned for survival and self-protection, disempowering the negative ego that has become so powerful. This has to happen in order to peel back the layers that keep us continually turning away from our true selves at the beck and call of our egos. True meaning is found by mixing the ingredients of heart-centeredness, wise mind, healthy tamed ego, a strong sense of self, connection, compassion, kindness, acceptance, knowing, Truth and a desire for good. **What I Know to Be True is that a return to this way of being brings meaning and purpose to our lives.**

It all begins with Awareness

While it may feel as if the work of being human is an impossible task; that we all have a tremendous amount of work to do on ourselves–and we do–it doesn't have to be as hard as it appears. We tend to make things harder than they have to be and we often take ourselves too seriously. It doesn't have to take years of therapy or a solitary, silent retreat, although those certainly may help. It just starts with the first step of awareness; noticing what had previously gone unnoticed. As awareness grows, so does the soul's desire for Truth. Before long you will see and feel differently.

When you choose to no longer operate in unconscious default mode, negativity towards self and others will start to feel more uncomfortable than it did previously. You will find yourself fixating less on negative thoughts as you make the decision to focus on the positive. Suffering will dissipate faster, causing you to bounce back quicker than usual. Finding the humor in the experience will allow you to watch how others lighten up when you do. What once took concentrated effort will soon flow more easily as your soul pushes you faster towards alignment with your Truth. And *What I Know to Be True* is that when we feel secure, in ourselves, our relationships, our place in the world, we will then open our hearts without fear and our lives will open up in ways we never anticipated.

You are the Gateway

⌀

What I Know to Be True is the Key

Look *in here* for what you seek out there

The search for happiness and inner peace is a universal one, but we tend to see it as something outside ourselves; something we are always seeking but which remains elusive and outside our grasp. We are looking for it in the wrong place. There is no "out there" to provide the answers to our problems. Not only are *You* the gateway itself, but you hold the *Key* to open the gate. *What I **Know** to Be True is* that key. In other words, you can only see and reach that expansive place of possibility by going first *through* the gateway that is deep within you. In order to get "there," you have first to go "here."

This is at the heart of many spiritual practices, for example being on the mat in yoga or sitting in meditation. The beauty of this lies in its simplicity. In order to open up to the limitless, expansive place you seek, you have only to focus on moving through the center that is *You*. Envision yourself holding the key to the gateway that opens you up to universal wellbeing. Use the key to open the gateway and look within to the space that awaits you.

You are the Gateway, *What I **Know** to Be True* is the Key.

From the personal to the more universal

Sometimes you will feel painful emotions. Period. Accepting this and recognizing that you can choose to walk out of the darkness towards the light that is you, will change your perspective and open your eyes to the support and possibility that await you within. Relief is found by looking towards yourself, not by turning away.

You may notice in your own practice of *What I **Know** to Be True*, as well as in the examples we offer, how often the *What I **Know** to Be True* statements to which you are connecting progress from the very personal to the more universal in nature. As you go within, you will feel the ever-expanding sense of detaching from the emotions associated with your experience and find yourself connecting to something bigger.

Getting comfortable with your discomfort

The challenge exists in getting comfortable with your discomfort, without either being consumed by it or running away from it, but rather using it as the cue to turn towards yourself and the universe for help. You will learn to trust that stepping through your inner gateway of Self opens you to an expansive space filled with light, ease and relief from the emotions and negativity that previously consumed you. The deeper and more automatic your practice becomes, the shorter your pathway to that space. **What I Know to Be True can put a stop to the all-consuming nature of your emotions, allowing you to be filled instead with connection, divine guidance, joy and ease.**

Take a look at it for yourself. Think of an example of a personal problem where you found yourself spiraling into the depths of pain, fear or anxiety. See how very small your world became, and how you may have felt completely consumed by it. Imagine if you had been able to stop the flow of negative energy by pausing, turning back towards yourself and trusting that, not only are you able to stop the flood, but also that you can redirect yourself to the gateway that offers relief—the gateway of Self to which you hold the key. **What I Know to Be True brings you a new and different perspective.**

Stepping into Your Light

Each of us is a powerful force of energy, a conduit for the healing change we wish to see in the world. Staying connected to our Truth reminds us to hold ourselves in the very highest of esteem, whatever our life's purpose may appear to be, trusting that our very existence signals a calling greater than we can ever know. When we lift the veil that falls like a curtain between us and our very best self, new horizons show themselves to us. Using *What I **Know** to Be True* as a way to step fully into our power, our Truth, our Light, we will shine even brighter than we do already, one bright star in a galaxy of many.

Aligning more closely with our Truth each and every day will not only break through the fear to change our own lives, but will affect the lives of many on the planet. We are both a teacher and a student of the bigger universe. **What I *Know* to Be True is that by being aware of, and trusting, the integral part I play in the greater whole, I give myself permission to hold myself in the highest of esteem and let the world see me in a new light.**

The Seed

What lies within, waiting to emerge,
there, a timeless knowing

Born with this knowledge, we grow to fill the
space around

With life, weaving its patterns, some we create,
some we are given

Slowly, we begin to *feel* a stirring, a spark that
ignites our true spirit

Returning to the source, where all began, we create
again from our own seed.

Cindy Marcus

What I Know to Be True:
The Practice

We tend to become so "hooked" into the stories–or illusions–created by our egos that we spend much of our time living in self-judgment, regret about the past, fear of the future, or even just trying to be "right." In reality, they are only stories made up in our heads. Trust that your True nature is better equipped to seek and *Know* your Truth, than your ego.

The relief that comes from tapping into your own Truth is found by meeting yourself in the mirror and turning towards, not away from, all that you see–your pain, your joy, your failures, your successes–with honesty, compassion and understanding. The relief comes from finding a way to accept, and live in peace with, the simple reality of your life, full of both joy and suffering. When your emotional mind threatens to overwhelm you, scare you, and makes you want to either run away or immediately "fix" the problem (both forms of escapism which send you spiraling further out of control), stepping back and observing yourself can make all the difference.

We suggest that you meet yourself in that place of your own awareness, with a soft heart. You will start to notice how and when your emotions threaten to engulf you, and become aware of the triggers within you that set off an emotional reaction. With the help of *What I **Know** to Be True*, you will find relief and transform your experiences. By being in your own presence in Truth, you disempower your negative ego voice and access the ultimate support that you can completely count on. You will meet each moment with the loving kindness of a trusted friend and teacher.

What I **Know** to Be True is an energetic practice. Trust that it will help you reconnect with your inner wisdom, your higher self, your ultimate Source. Use the words What I *Know* to Be True as the key to that connection. These words are a catalyst that allow your mind to access its True wisdom and connect with your heart. Visualize the heart space where wisdom happens, and the pause in your mind's chatter, carved out by the words What I *Know* to Be True. Visualize the words as a key to open the door into your inner wisdom.

Using the practice of *What I* **Know** *to Be True*, you will walk onto a new path of inner peace by connecting more fully and more often with your innate wisdom—that tuned-in gut feeling of knowing that we so often ignore. The message brought to you through *What I* **Know** *to Be True* is one of wisdom and, as importantly, compassion, to support you along the way.

What I **Know** *to Be True* helps you to get more in touch with the *experience* that happens through practice, beyond cognition. *Feeling* the rewards of the change provides the incentive to look for more of what you seek at heart. The key is to practice. Practice is how you learn—like learning to ride a bike or read a book. There are very few things that are learned without repetition. Connection with your Truth is cultivated in the same way.

As with anything new, you are likely to meet with resistance along the way, resistance in the form of fear messages that tell you "you can't." Acknowledge the resistance and take a step anyway. Like exercising a muscle at the gym, living in Truth will get easier with practice and habit. The more you use *What I* **Know** *to Be True*, the easier and more automatic it becomes.

Our hope is that you will use the experience of this practice to explore your journey and live your life in a more conscious, deliberate way, using *What I **Know** to Be True* to help you. What we Know to Be True is that when you say these words—"What I *Know* to Be True" aloud and often—you begin to deeply *feel* the effect of tapping into your own Truth rather than someone else's truth for your life. Listen to yourself and the knowing voice inside you, trust in yourself and create a relationship with your True self; that aspect of yourself that is always love, compassion, security and safety, no matter what is going on around you. Whatever challenges you face, you will be happier if you are being True to who you really are. *What I **Know** to Be True* is the seed. Nourish it and watch it grow.

You can use *What I **Know** to Be True* at any time, in any place, and without anyone else knowing. How you use the practice of *What I **Know** to Be True* is entirely up to you. While we don't want to provide you with answers that are not *your* own truth, we offer you guidance and suggestions for how using *What I **Know** to Be True* may be helpful, and which may set you on the right path—*your* path. It is up to you to discover what is true for you. If what we share doesn't resonate for you, let it go and tune in to your own guidance. Find your own way to your Truth. When you tap into your own Truth, you will feel it.

To Feel the Truth is Transformative

How do we know when we've tapped into our Truth? We *feel* our way into it.

Have you ever had the experience of just knowing something? Someone asked you a question or you had to make a decision for yourself and the answer was somehow just right there at hand—there was simply no question in your mind. You couldn't necessarily explain it, you just *knew* in your heart and soul.

When you are tapped into your Truth you will *feel* it. Knowing something in your head is informative; but *feeling* it in your body is where the transformation occurs. It may show up as a gut feeling, a tingling, a flash of heat or light, or simply a sense of completeness, of wholeness. It is the 'ahhh" moment when you just know something is right. Honing your awareness through the practice of *What I Know to Be True* will help you recognize what is true for you instantly when you *feel* it. It will shine a light on illusions you have created.

It helps to close your eyes and get quiet, or to meditate for more profound insight and confirmation. The simple act of closing your eyes shades the distractions, quiets your mind and allows you to pause, breathe and bring your focus inward. Listen for your inner wisdom. A quiet confidence will blossom as you begin to know and trust the *feeling* of being tapped into your Truth. **What I Know to Be True is that my soul Truth, the Truth that I feel in my body, needs no validation.**

~Practice anywhere and any time you find an opportunity; it will become that much easier during a truly challenging time~

~SIX SIMPLE STEPS TO SET YOU FREE~

NOTICE the cues from your thoughts,
your feelings, and your body.
*"I need to pay immediate attention to
the messages I am getting."*

PAUSE & take several deep breaths to
settle your emotional energy.
*"I can use my breath to slow myself down
and turn my attention inward."*

USE the words **What I Know to Be True** to
detach from whatever emotion is consuming
you and to connect with your Truth.
*"Even though I'm feeling…. What I **Know** to Be True is …."*

NOTICE the space that arises in which you
can choose to respond differently.
*"I feel empowered and supportive of myself
when I choose a new response."*

FEEL the relief.
ACKNOWLEDGE & CELEBRATE
What You Know to Be True

Give yourself a Hug~

Use *What I Know to Be True* to SOOTHE YOURSELF when your emotions threaten to overwhelm you

Use *What I Know to Be True* when your emotional mind threatens to envelop you, causing you to react without thinking. If left untended, your emotions can hijack you, leaving you feeling reactive and out of control. There may be a strong sense of fear involved. The feelings in your body that alert you to the hijacking are the cues you need to recognize what is happening. This is your prompt to pause, take some deep breaths to soothe the emotions so you can access your rational mind and choose a grounded response.

What I Know to Be True helps you quiet the powerful emotional response and tap into your wisdom before you spiral out of control with old reactive habits.

Pause…Breathe…

What I Know to Be True helps you to *respond*, rather than react.

+ *What I Know to Be True is that my emotions are real, however I am not my overwhelming emotion.*

+ *What I Know to Be True is that there may be fear behind the emotion I am feeling.*

+ *What I Know to Be True is that when I am tapped into my core, I can observe and tolerate these strong emotions without becoming consumed by them.*

+ *What I Know to Be True is that I am best served by settling my reactive emotional energy before responding.*

- *What I **Know** to Be True is that if I pause, breathe and feel the emotion, I can move right through it.*

- *What I **Know** to Be True is that I can acknowledge, allow, embrace and then let go of the overwhelming emotion.*

- *What I **Know** to Be True is that my emotions do not have to define my reality.*

- *What I **Know** to Be True is that fear is real but Love is bigger than the fear.*

- *What I **Know** to Be True is that I am never truly alone.*

Use *What I* **Know** *to Be True*
to find relief from MENTAL CHATTER

Too much mental chatter leads to overwhelm, which in turn leads to anxiety, stress and more overwhelm, unless you stop the spiraling thoughts. Mental chatter only serves to empower the mind, taking you away from your "being" self into a world of to-do lists and over-analyzing. It often reflects the perception that there is not enough time, money or ability to handle day-to-day needs. We doubt ourselves, question our decisions, strive to do more and more.

What I **Know** *to Be True* helps you move to a more heart-centered place where you can connect with a never-ending flow of serenity and resources, and where you remember what is of real significance. *Know* that relief comes in the stillness of being.

+ *What I **Know** to Be True is that when I relax and focus on this moment, rather than projecting ahead, I will find that I have all the time I need.*

+ *What I **Know** to Be True is that when I focus on what is truly important to me, I can prioritize my activities and not feel like I need to do it all.*

+ *What I **Know** to Be True is that when I embrace the overwhelm, rather than resist it, I can relax and become more productive.*

+ *What I **Know** Be True is that when I focus on what is truly important to me, I can prioritize my activities and not feel like I need to do it all.*

+ *What I **Know** to Be True is that when I let go of what others think, I let go of the need to do everything perfectly.*

+ *What I **Know** to Be True is that when I pause and make a decision from my centered self, I can stop questioning myself and trust that it will be the right decision for me.*

+ *What I **Know** to Be True is that when I surrender and allow things to unfold, I can let go of the illusion that I am responsible for everything.*

+ *What I **Know** to Be True is that when I detach from the mental chatter and go within, I can hear my heart wisdom.*

Use *What I* **Know** *to Be True*
to SHIFT NEGATIVE THOUGHTS

Use *What I* **Know** *to Be True* when you are having difficulty controlling your spiraling negative thoughts. It will help you stop the old tape of negative self-talk that leads to more negative self-talk, and so on. It will realign you with your center, enabling you to access the more positive state of ease found in Truth.

+ *What I* **Know** *to Be True is that my thoughts create my reality.*

+ *What I* **Know** *to Be True is that I can choose different thoughts to change my reality.*

+ *What I* **Know** *to Be True is that I can let go of thoughts that come from ego.*

+ *What I* **Know** *to Be True is that shifting my thoughts one at a time will shift everything.*

+ *What I* **Know** *to Be True is that choosing positive thoughts creates positive outcomes.*

+ *What I* **Know** *to Be True is that I can choose a new narrative for myself.*

NOTICE the cues from your thoughts,
your feelings, and your body.
*"I need to pay immediate attention to
the messages I am getting."*

PAUSE & take several deep breaths to
settle your emotional energy.
*"I can use my breath to slow myself down
and turn my attention inward."*

USE the words **What I Know to Be True** to
detach from whatever emotion is consuming
you and to connect with your Truth.
*"Even though I'm feeling…. What I **Know** to Be True is …."*

NOTICE the space that arises in which you
can choose to respond differently.
*"I feel empowered and supportive of myself
when I choose a new response."*

FEEL the relief.

ACKNOWLEDGE & CELEBRATE
What You Know to Be True

Use *What I* **Know** *to Be True* in **STRESSFUL SITUATIONS**

You encounter stressful situations each and every day, large and small. In traffic jams, long lines, any time you feel out of control or when things are not going the way you had planned. You may be in a stressful work situation where you are feeling pressured. Use *What I* **Know** *to Be True* in these situations and notice how you feel.

+ *What I* **Know** *to Be True is that while I cannot control this situation, I can control my reaction to it.*

+ *What I* **Know** *to Be True is that I can ease the stress by not resisting the circumstances, which I cannot control.*

+ *What I* **Know** *to Be True is that when I let go of having to be right, things usually work out.*

+ *What I* **Know** *to Be True is that when I surrender the need to be perfect, my life will be less stressful.*

+ *What I* **Know** *to Be True is that when I look at the situation from a bird's eye view I can gain greater clarity.*

+ *What I* **Know** *to Be True is that if I know I am as prepared as possible and do my best, I can let go of the outcome.*

+ *What I* **Know** *to Be True is that I have time for everything and all will be well.*

+ *What I* **Know** *to Be True is that time spent waiting is an opportunity to just be with myself.*

Use *What I* **Know** *to Be True* to provide RELIEF FROM PHYSICAL PAIN

Tapping into your essence, your Truth, when you are in physical pain relieves the focus on the pain which, in turn, diminishes the actual pain. Instead of focusing on the pain, thereby feeding it, gently acknowledge the pain and divert your attention to *What You* **Know** *to Be True*. While physical pain can be real, when you tap into your **knowing** that all is well, you bring healing energy to your body.

You may want to place your hand gently on your body where it is in pain, while saying to yourself…

Even though I am in physical pain,

+ *What I* **Know** *to Be True is that focusing on the pain will only increase it.*

+ *What I* **Know** *to Be True is that the pain is a messenger, if only I can listen to it and not fear it.*

+ *What I* **Know** *to Be True is that my body needs loving support and healing energy when it is hurting.*

+ *What I* **Know** *to Be True is that I can control my frightened thoughts and not attach negative meaning to the pain.*

+ *What I* **Know** *to Be True is that I am not alone and can seek help at any time.*

+ *What I* **Know** *to Be True is that all is well.*

Use *What I* **Know** *to Be True* to help **DIFFUSE CONFLICT**

Use the words *What I* **Know** *to Be True* when in conflict with another person. Prefacing your statements or responses with these words helps detach the emotion from the language, which in turn helps the other person hear that you are speaking your own Truth and not their Truth.

To feel angry from time to time is natural, but to act on it and engage in battle feeds our need to be right and to win. Things are seldom black or white, but rather various shades of grey. Mindful and compassionate communication, using *What I* **Know** *to Be True*, keeps you aware of the vulnerability present in both parties and allows you to respond differently. The result is win-win, even if you disagree.

+ *What I* **Know** *to Be True is that I am feeling (identify emotion) about the conflict we are experiencing.*

+ *What I* **Know** *to Be True is that I hear your pain and I am hurting as well.*

+ *What I* **Know** *to Be True is that I am asking you to hear my pain.*

+ *What I* **Know** *to Be True is this isn't really about me or you but about our own individual Truths.*

+ *What I* **Know** *to Be True is that I can release the need to be right and still be true to myself.*

+ *What I* **Know** *to Be True is that each of us having our own Truth doesn't make the other wrong.*

+ *What I* **Know** *to Be True is that we can step back from the issue in order to see our way to resolving it.*

Use *What I* **Know** *to Be True* with your PARTNER or CHILD

Use *What I* **Know** *to Be True* when you are at odds with your partner or child. It will help you to reaffirm your love for each other and to settle any tension you are feeling between you.

+ *What I* **Know** *to Be True is that I love my partner/child unconditionally.*

+ *What I* **Know** *to Be True is that it is okay to disagree.*

+ *What I* **Know** *to Be True is that if I come from love, my response will be healing and connecting.*

+ *What I* **Know** *to Be True is that learning to speak my truth and to listen to the truth of another will make our relationship more fulfilling.*

+ *What I* **Know** *to Be True is that when I explain calmly and quietly to my partner/child the reasons behind the emotions, he/she will not take it so personally.*

+ *What I* **Know** *to Be True is that my partner/child needs to create their own definition of success, not one that I impose.*

+ *What I* **Know** *to Be True is that my role is to provide a secure foundation for my child until she/he can do so for themselves.*

+ *What I* **Know** *to Be True is that my partner/child are on their own journey, not mine.*

+ *What I **Know** to Be True is that I can tolerate my emotions without taking it out on those I love.*

+ *What I **Know** to Be True is that I have all the patience I need.*

+ *What I **Know** to Be True is the best thing to do is wrap the other person in love.*

Use *What I **Know** to Be True*
to help with DECISION MAKING

Making a decision can be difficult. You may be swayed by what others think, or wonder if you will make the right decision. Tapping into your Truth helps you realize that a decision is just a decision—the best you know how to make at the time. You are then supported from a centered place, trusting in your own Truth, and allowing you to align with the decision and move forward.

+ *What I **Know** to Be True is that there is no right or wrong choice.*

+ *What I **Know** to Be True is that what matters most is that I fully commit to the decision with my heart.*

+ *What I **Know** to Be True is that when I tap into my core, I will know the answer.*

+ *What I **Know** to Be True is that I'm making the best decision I can for myself in this moment.*

+ *What I **Know** to Be True is that no one else knows what is best for me.*

Use *What I* **Know** *to Be True* upon WAKING

Use *What I* **Know** *to Be True* as an affirmation in the morning. Affirmations welcome in the new.

Take a few moments to ease gently into the day by setting your intentions. For example,

+ *What I* **Know** *to Be True is that I set my intention for my day to be fulfilling.*

+ *What I* **Know** *to Be True is that I will have all the time I need today.*

+ *What I* **Know** *to Be True is that my activities will flow with grace and ease throughout the day.*

+ *What I* **Know** *to Be True is that today I will be kind and gentle towards myself and others.*

+ *What I* **Know** *to Be True is that I will do one thing that makes me happy before doing what I "have" to.*

+ *What I* **Know** *to Be True is that everything is in perfect order for me today.*

Use *What I Know* to Be True
to JOURNAL

Use *What I Know to Be True* as a way of expressing yourself in writing. Writing allows you to witness yourself in slow motion, to privately break down your thoughts and your feelings. It helps bring clarity and allows you to truly "see" yourself.

Write the words "What I *Know* to Be True is..." and allow yourself to write whatever comes. You may want to do a short centering exercise before beginning by closing your eyes, taking a deep breath, and asking for your higher self and your guides to give you the words. Do not judge it, just allow it. Bring patience and love to the process. Put it away and go back to it. Let go and see yourself wherever you are.

+ *What I **Know** to Be True is that when I express myself in writing it helps me connect with my core, my truth.*

+ *What I **Know** to Be True is that when I write, it helps me detach from the emotions and gain perspective and clarity.*

+ *What I **Know** to Be True is that writing allows me to share my feelings with the universe and not keep them inside.*

+ *What I **Know** to Be True is that writing helps me to separate from my story.*

Use *What I **Know** to Be True* to help you SLEEP

The busier your mind and your life become, the harder it is to shut down at night and give in to the blissful reprieve of restful sleep. *What I **Know** to Be True* can help the transition from being awake to sleeping. Close your eyes and rest your head on the pillow. As you start to relax from the energy and stresses of your day, use *What I **Know** to Be True* to ease your passage into sleep.

+ *What I **Know** to Be True is that the stresses of my day are not reflective of my truth; stress is just stress.*

+ *What I **Know** to Be True is that I choose to release the anxieties and worries of the day.*

+ *What I **Know** to Be True is that I can set my intention for a fully restful sleep.*

+ *What I **Know** to Be True is that I send loving energy to myself and my loved ones.*

+ *What I **Know** to Be True is that I deserve a restful and rejuvenating sleep*

+ *What I **Know** to Be True is that I can rest tonight knowing that a power greater than me is keeping me safe.*

Use *What I **Know** to Be True* to find the Balance Between HEART & MIND

Part of the energetic shift occurring in the world at this time is one of creating a more balanced connection between our hearts and our heads. This means giving more credibility to our heart wisdom than ever before and creating a new relationship between the two.

Notice the balance between your heart and mind and become aware of any adjustments you would like to make. Use *What I Know to Be True* to create that new connection.

+ *What I **Know** to Be True is that my head doesn't have all the answers.*

+ *What I **Know** to Be True is that my heart doesn't have all the answers.*

+ *What I **Know** to Be True is that I can listen to what my mind tells me and then check in with what my heart says.*

+ *What I **Know** to Be True is that I can feel my emotions clearly and then pause to shift my thoughts.*

+ *What I **Know** to Be True is that when I'm connected with my Truth, my mind and heart are in balance.*

+ *What I **Know** to Be True is that true wisdom is accessed through my heart.*

Use Meditation to Deepen Your Experience

It is impossible to write about how to live a more conscious, happier and peaceful life without addressing the topic of meditation, especially since *What I Know to Be True* was birthed during meditation. Establishing a regular meditation practice will deepen your experience of using *What I Know to Be True*, helping you to drop quicker and more easily into the still space that delivers the true wisdom from within.

Numerous studies have been done, all of which show exponential benefits from meditation. It even changes the way our brains work, promising to increase our focus, boost our immune system, lengthen our lives, improve our creativity and problem solving abilities, help us to make better decisions, reduce anxiety and depression — the list goes on.

Ask the question "What do I want to BE more of in this life?" and the answer is inevitably "happier, more peaceful, free, more loved, compassionate, etc." All of these feeling states are attainable through meditation, whatever unrest appears to be going on in your daily life.

The busier we are, the more we resist meditating as it requires us to slow down, stop and become quiet. The irony, of course, is that regular meditation actually allows us to accomplish more, and with less stress if we just give ourselves the gift of a few moments each day.

The myth we often hold onto is that we are not capable of quieting our mind. However, meditation isn't really about quieting the mind, but rather about allowing and becoming conscious of thoughts flowing. The more we become conscious of the thoughts, the more we can decide to let them go. The more we let them go, the easier it is to tap into the stillness that already exists in each one of us.

Being mindful means becoming and being more conscious by noticing what previously went unnoticed. Meditation allows us to tap into consciousness itself. *What I Know to Be True* provides a shortcut to consciousness, helping you tap into the space within more quickly and easily. The more you practice, the deeper and more profound the connection with your Truth, and the happier your life will be.

Practice Finding Peace
from the Inside Out

Finding Peace from the Inside Out is a **guided meditation**. It's helpful to familiarize yourself with this exercise by reading it aloud fully several times before meditating. Read it slowly and pause often. You may prefer to download a free podcast of the meditation from our website. Listening to it on a regular basis will hone your ability to tap into your core at will informally, any time, any place.

> *Find a quiet place that feels safe for you, one where you won't be interrupted and gently allow your eyes to close. Rest for a few minutes allowing yourself to become at one with the rhythm of your breath, noticing how your energy settles naturally when you do so. Invite yourself to relax. You have no place to go, nothing to do, just be here now. Use your breath as a way to slow down and ground yourself.*
>
> *Breath in…Breath out…*
>
> *Breath in…Breath out…*
>
> *PAUSE…*
>
> *If your mind becomes busy, as it may well do, just allow the thoughts to float there outside of yourself without reaching for them, and bring your attention back to the natural rhythm of your body breathing. They are just thoughts, nothing more. Choose only to witness them, then let them go. Meet yourself wherever you are and feel the support of your own presence there.*

PAUSE...

Perhaps you want to set an intention for your meditation time today.

PAUSE…

Imagine yourself as a tiny, but important, piece of a huge universal puzzle. Feel yourself connect to that energy. Trust what you are sensing as you drop deeper in the feeling of being a part of something bigger. Imagine yourself just floating effortlessly in the space without filling it. Allow yourself to feel the sensation of melting into your surroundings, into your senses, both inside of yourself and out, beyond time and space.

PAUSE…

From this place of expanded awareness, drop into the center of yourself and identify any current issue that is troubling you. Allow any emotion or feeling attached to this issue to surface without judging or censoring it, just noticing with idle curiosity.

PAUSE…

Notice where in your body you feel the emotion and focus your attention there, inviting tenderness and love to that space within. Connect with the feeling of compassion and softness. Breathe deeply and gently into that physical space in your body.

Breath in…Breath out…

Breath in…Breath out…

PAUSE...

*Start quietly repeating the mantra "What I **Know** to Be True" to yourself.*

*"What I **Know** to Be True is..." (pause)*

*"What I **Know** to Be True is..." (pause)*

*"What I **Know** to Be True is..." (pause)*

*Allow your Truth to naturally complete the sentence with what your inner core tells you. "What I **Know** to Be True is..." Don't censor or question, allow whatever comes.*

*[If the initial response feels negative, look again. Your true inner wisdom will only provide positive insights. There is no predetermined number of What I **Know** to Be True prompts or responses; every situation is different.]*

*Notice how your body feels; listen for that confirmation, listen well. Allow yourself to feel that Truth, to feel any physical indication in your body. If you find yourself distracted, gently bring yourself back to the rhythm of your breath and the words "What I **Know** to Be True."*

PAUSE...

Imagine your heart expanding and opening as you go inward to your own Truth while at the same time expanding outward into a greater awareness of the larger universe of which you are but a small part.

Rest there a while, suspended in the space in between, just being and listening.

PAUSE…

Whenever you are ready, bring your attention back into your physical body, wiggling your fingers and toes, stretching, and gradually, in your own time, coming back into your body. Bow your head slightly and gently allow your eyes to fall open without fully focusing before lifting your head and taking time to refocus your gaze back into this time and space, into the room. Take a deep breath and acknowledge the gift you have given yourself.

+ There is no minimum and no limit to the number of *What I **Know** to Be True* insights that arise; do what feels right for you.

+ Trust that you will know when to stop for now.

+ Acknowledge and celebrate what you **know** to be true. Give yourself a hug.

You may want to capture your insights in writing. Use them as a reference to continue the exploration of your Truth or as a reminder, when needed.

*What I **Know** to Be True* is that you can return to this place at any time, seeking and finding peace from the only place that really matters—that of your own Truth.

Icon Meditation

The icon used throughout the book provides another opportunity for meditation.

Focus on the image of the icon as a way to connect to the quiet within. You can do this silently or while listening to the guided meditation accessed through our website.

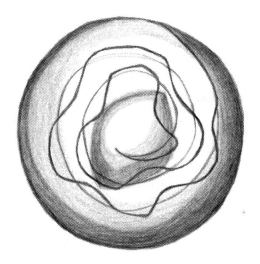

*"This icon, energetically created to capture the essence of What I **Know** to Be True, visually expresses the journey a person takes using What I **Know** to Be True." ~Anna Linley, Intuitive Artist*

Use *What I **Know** to Be True*
to REMEMBER YOUR TRUTH

Use *What I **Know** to Be True* to remember the Truth about yourself, whatever that might be. You have the Key to open the door to a happier, more peaceful and truthful relationship with yourself, others and the world you live in.

- *What I **Know** to Be True is that what I seek I already know.*

- *What I **Know** to Be True is that I can change my thoughts to create a new reality.*

- *What I **Know** to Be True is that when I think positive thoughts, I feel better.*

- *What I **Know** to Be True is that when I feel better I can create the life I want and deserve.*

- *What I **Know** to Be True is that when I don't take on the emotions of others, I can stay centered and remain true to myself.*

- *What I **Know** to Be True is that one day can make all the difference in the world.*

- *What I **Know** to Be True is when I tap into my core I connect with my true self, my unequivocal Truth.*

- *What I **Know** to Be True is that when I tap into my core I stay connected to that aspect of myself that is always love, compassion, strength and security.*

Reminder to Practice

~SIX SIMPLE STEPS TO SET YOU FREE~

NOTICE the cues from your thoughts,
your feelings, and your body.
"I need to pay immediate attention to the messages I am getting."

PAUSE & take several deep breaths to
settle your emotional energy."
*I can use my breath to slow myself down
and turn my attention inward."*

USE the words **What I Know to Be True** to
detach from whatever emotion is consuming
you and to connect with your Truth.
*"Even though I'm feeling.... What I **Know** to Be True is ...."*

NOTICE the space that arises in which you
can choose to respond differently.
*"I feel empowered and supportive of myself
when I choose a new response."*

FEEL the relief.

ACKNOWLEDGE & CELEBRATE
What You Know to Be True
Give yourself a Hug~

What I Know to Be True Truisms

On the pages that follow you will find guidance in the form of what we are calling "**Truisms**" to help you apply the concept of *What I Know to Be True*. These practices range from the very simple to the more profound relationship with yourself and the words "What I *Know* to Be True."

Such Truisms are the natural result of a deepening practice of *What I Know to Be True*, and as such, you may find yourself capturing your own. In the meantime, the **Truisms** we have captured from our own experiences may act as reminders, they may resonate strongly for you, and they may awaken your curiosity. They may ring true to you as-is, or you may want to tweak them to suit your own Truth. That is for you to decide. You are both your own student and teacher.

Many of the Truisms offer an opportunity to practice different ways of using *What I Know to Be True*. Each Truism stands alone, while at the same time, each is part of a powerful, transformational collective. Read and use them in the way that feels right for you. Regular repetition of the practice is the best way to shift to living your life from a centered, conscious place of your Truth.

What I Know to Be True

WHAT I KNOW TO BE TRUE
IS THAT MY OWN TRUTH IS WHAT
MATTERS MOST.

When I operate from the premise that what
someone else says is true for me, the peace
and happiness I seek will elude me. When I
connect with my own Truth, my own Knowing,
I live in a place of integrity and clarity,
regardless of the response from others.

Universal Knowing

WHAT I KNOW TO BE TRUE
IS THAT EVERYTHING THAT HAPPENS
IN MY LIFE IS AN OPPORTUNITY
FOR MY SPIRITUAL GROWTH.

If I can accept that everything that happens serves a higher purpose for good, I can stop asking, "Why did this happen?" and "How do I fix this?"

Things are exactly the way they're meant to be.

Universal Knowing

WHAT I KNOW TO BE TRUE
IS THAT SPIRIT IS EVERYWHERE
AND IN EVERYTHING.

When I truly "see" all that is around
me, I am aware of the energy of life in
all things, the Source energy that has
created all that I am and all that I know.

Universal Knowing

What I Know to Be True
IS THAT UNIVERSAL TRUTHS ARE SIMPLE.

Humans tend to complicate things. When I am able to cut through the layers of resistance to the Truth, I find simplicity. When I strip away the beliefs, the emotions, the drama, the answers come to me in the simplest of terms.

Universal Knowing

WHAT I KNOW TO BE TRUE
IS THAT LOVE IS EVERYTHING.

With love, I remember who I am. Everything changes when I come from love.

Universal Knowing

WHAT I KNOW TO BE TRUE
IS THAT PURE LOVE IS UNCONDITIONAL.

There are many kinds of love. Sometimes when I believe I am coming from love, I may in fact be acting out of need.

Unconditional love comes without strings or expectations. *What I **Know** to Be True* helps me to tap into that unconditional love.

Universal Knowing

WHAT I KNOW TO BE TRUE
IS THAT WHAT I THINK I KNOW IS ONLY
A TINY PART OF WHAT I KNOW.

What I know of reality in this human form is infinitesimal; I cannot fully comprehend all that my brain is capable of.

What I **Know** is unlimited, a Knowing from Source, Spirit, All-there-is, where I have access to all Universal knowledge.

Universal Knowing

WHAT I KNOW TO BE TRUE
IS THAT I HAVE ALL THE KNOWING AND
TRUTH I NEED HERE INSIDE MYSELF.

Wordless knowledge is when I listen to my intuition, my gut feeling or my heart, as opposed to my head. Whatever I choose to call it, this is the place I can best reach in quiet meditation.

By sitting within myself in stillness and tapping into my core, I find the guidance and answers that are right for me.

We invite you to sit quietly with yourself for five minutes and listen to your heart wisdom.

Universal Knowing

What I Know to Be True
allows me to find my own path.

———

Greater awareness provides me with
an opportunity to stay on my own path
rather than follow a path that may
have been set out for me by others.

*What I **Know** to Be True* helps me tap into
my own truth, not someone else's truth for
me. The more I practice listening to my own
inner wisdom, the more I learn to trust it.

Creation

WHAT I KNOW TO BE TRUE
IS THAT ALL CREATION IS
BORN OUT OF DESIRE.

Desire is the seed for the creation of my deepest wishes. My life is continuously unfolding, based on the intention I send to the Universe.

When I connect with my Truth, I can access my heart's desires and plant the seeds for my deepest wishes to be met.

Creation

WHAT I KNOW TO BE TRUE
IS THAT THE ENERGY OF MANIFESTING
MY DESIRES BEGINS WITH A RESOUNDING
"YES" FROM WITHIN ME.

When I hold the space in this very moment
to feel the support of my own presence,
I manifest the energy that will propel
me toward that which I desire. It is the
energy in each moment, not the goal,
which leads me toward my dreams.

Creation

WHAT I KNOW TO BE TRUE
IS THAT I CAN CREATE A VISION FOR
HOW I WANT MY LIFE TO BE.

If I want to be happy, I need to focus on what makes me happy. Taking small action steps daily towards my vision helps me co-create my new reality.

Creation

WHAT I KNOW TO BE TRUE
IS THAT WHICH I TURN MY
ATTENTION TO GROWS.

Everything requires nourishment in order
to survive and thrive. Whatever I focus my
energy on expands, including the undesirable.

"I choose carefully where I focus
my thoughts and attention."

Creation

WHAT I KNOW TO BE TRUE
IS THAT I CAN MANIFEST MY DESIRE WITH
THE USE OF INTENTION AND ATTENTION.

Setting an intention means using the power of my mind to fulfill a desire. These desires–or intentions–will then need nourishment and attention in order to expand and grow.

LISA JACOBY & CAROLINE J TEMPLE

Thoughts/Beliefs

WHAT I KNOW TO BE TRUE
IS THAT I CREATE MY OWN REALITY
BY CHOOSING MY THOUGHTS.

I must be conscious and present enough
to choose what thoughts I attend to. I can
create my thoughts rather than allowing my
thoughts to rule me. The negative chatter
and narrative I create in my mind, and the
subsequent conclusions I draw, will only serve
to reinforce old, negative beliefs and patterns.

*What I **Know** to Be True* is the gateway
to a new narrative and a new reality.

Thoughts/Beliefs

WHAT I KNOW TO BE TRUE
IS THAT WHILE MY THOUGHTS CREATE
MY REALITY, I AM NOT MY THOUGHTS.

My thoughts do not define me,
therefore I can choose to believe
them or choose a different reality.

"I notice my patterns of negative thinking
and choose to shift my thoughts."

Thoughts/Beliefs

WHAT I KNOW TO BE TRUE
IS THAT WHEN I AM CAREFUL WITH MY
WORDS, MY THOUGHTS WILL CHANGE
AND NEW ACTIONS WILL FOLLOW.

It starts with the words I choose to use. When I am mindful of what I say, especially to myself, I can then more easily change my thoughts to become more positive, productive, and empowering. Then actions follow thought.

Thoughts/Beliefs

WHAT I KNOW TO BE TRUE
IS THAT I AM NOT MY BELIEFS AND
MY BELIEFS ARE NOT MY TRUTH.

Even though I may have unconsciously
internalized beliefs from society, peers, and
through the voices of childhood, I can trust
that I, and I alone, know where my truth lies.

When I tap into my own Truth I am able
to discern between what is learned
and *What I **Know** to Be True* for me.

Thoughts/Beliefs

WHAT I KNOW TO BE TRUE
CUTS THROUGH THE LAYERS OF BELIEF
SYSTEMS AND CHANGES MY OLD TAPES.

The term "knee-jerk reaction" paints
a picture of how our minds work:
instantaneous reactions that the mind has
been trained for, occurring over and over.

What I **Know** to Be True slices through the
looping tapes, interrupting the habitual
reflexes, to connect me directly with my
true source of wisdom and break the cycle.

Thoughts/Beliefs

WHAT I KNOW TO BE TRUE
IS THAT TO *KNOW* IS MORE
THAN TO BELIEVE.

Learned beliefs often give me a
false sense of who I am.

When I tap into *What I **Know** to Be True*, I
can access an inherent greater knowing
that resonates with every cell in my body.

Inner Peace

WHAT I KNOW TO BE TRUE
IS THAT WHEN I LET GO OF THE HOW'S" AND
"WHY'S" I CAN LIVE A HAPPIER,
MORE PEACEFUL LIFE.

Staying in the intellectual desire to know how and why only keeps me stuck, usually in anger, hurt or blame. In order to heal through a difficult situation, it helps if I stop asking "why?" and instead soothe myself through the challenging feelings that arise.

Inner Peace

WHAT I KNOW TO BE TRUE
IS THAT I CAN FIND INNER PEACE
BY EMBRACING AN ATTITUDE OF
ACCEPTANCE AND NON-JUDGMENT.

The inner peace and happiness I seek will continue to elude me when I resist each personal experience just as it is. I must learn to be gently present in the moment without judging it to be good or bad, right or wrong.

It is the path of non-resistance, acceptance and non-judgment that allows me to move through the pain I'm trying to escape.

"I accept events as they come, I accept people as they are and I accept life as it is. I stop trying to control things. I let go. I use these opportunities to learn and to grow."

Inner Peace

What I Know to Be True
is when i focus on creating a more
centered, peaceful and conscious life, i
live a life filled with grace and ease.

***

When I stop trying to escape "what is" and
let go of the need for distraction, I can live in
the here and now. My life is transformed.

What I **Know** to Be True helps me do just that.

Being Present

WHAT I KNOW TO BE TRUE
IS THAT I FEEL MORE AT PEACE
WHEN I LIVE IN THE PRESENT.

I can only live in the present moment.
It is my thoughts that take me back to
the past or forward to the future.

Choosing to live in the moment requires
courage and steadfastness to rest in the
place of "being" without trying to escape.

"I am present in the here and now".

Being Present

WHAT I KNOW TO BE TRUE
IS THAT THE MORE TIME I SPEND *BEING*
RATHER THAN DOING, THE MORE I
KNOW WHAT IS TRUE FOR ME.

Doing is often a distraction from being present with myself at any given moment, another form of escape. So often I create activity as a way to avoid being with myself. I often miss the significance of the moment because my mind is thinking of everything on my to-do list.

What I **Know** *to Be True* allows me to meet myself in the moment, regardless of the situation, fully experiencing all that life has to offer. *What I* **Know** *to Be True* teaches me tolerance to just sit with myself and be.

Being Present

WHAT I KNOW TO BE TRUE
IS THAT IF I SPEND TIME WITH MYSELF
QUIETLY, I WILL BECOME MORE OBSERVANT
AND ATTENTIVE TO MY OWN NEEDS.

Observe yourself for five minutes. Observe
the nature of your thoughts and how
they threaten to take you away from
the present. Notice habitual thinking,
discomfort, obsessions, without judgment.
Breathe into them with loving kindness.

*What I **Know** to Be True* helps me
settle back into the now.

We invite you to write about this experience.
Tomorrow stretch the first five minutes into
fifteen minutes, then into thirty minutes.
What does this feel like for you?

Being Present

WHAT I KNOW TO BE TRUE
IS THAT I CAN STAY WITH MYSELF IN THE
PRESENT, EVEN WHEN I'M HURTING.

The more I sit quietly with myself and
allow my feelings to surface, the more
I realize I can not only survive the pain
but work through to the other side.

Being Present

WHAT I KNOW TO BE TRUE
BRINGS ME BACK TO WHAT IS REAL AND
PRESENT IN THE HERE AND NOW.

The narrative (stories) I create, and
the conclusions I form in my mind,
distract me from the Truth, as does the
need to know "how" or "why".

I choose to focus only on the present moment.

Mindfulness

WHAT I KNOW TO BE TRUE
IS THAT I AM MORE PEACEFUL WHEN I
CHOOSE TO RESPOND FROM A CENTERED,
CLEAR PLACE, RATHER THAN REACT
EMOTIONALLY TO A SITUATION.

Do you ever get hooked by something going on outside of yourself? Something someone said or did? Hooks are everywhere; they catch us repeatedly and only lead to more drama and suffering.

Tapping into *What I **Know** to Be True* at the very moment of overwhelm can prevent me from being hooked by it, allowing me to respond from a place of clarity and strength.

*What I **Know** to Be True* allows me to float under the surface, resting in the calm waters, protected from the rage of the storm above.

Mindfulness

WHAT I KNOW TO BE TRUE
MAKES IT POSSIBLE FOR ME TO
ENDURE ANY CHALLENGING SITUATION
WITHOUT GETTING CONSUMED BY IT.

*What I **Know** to Be True* teaches me to stay centered and grounded in my own Truth even when I am overwhelmed by an emotion.

Mindfulness

What I Know to Be True
IS THAT I FIND GREATER CLARITY WHEN
I LEARN TO USE MY OBSERVING EYE ("I").

Development of the observing eye 'I' is key.
It allows me to step back from a situation
and observe myself lovingly, without
judgment. Just as a baby begins to realize
she is separate from her mother, I realize
that I am separate from my emotions.
I can choose to honor them, feel them,
acknowledge them, but not become them.

NOTICE the cues from your thoughts, your
feelings, and your body.
*"I need to pay immediate attention
to the messages I am getting."*

PAUSE & take several deep breaths to settle
your emotional energy.

*"I can use my breath to slow myself
down and turn my attention inward."*

USE the words **What I Know to Be True** to
detach from whatever emotion is consuming
you and to connect with your Truth.
*"Even though I'm feeling....
What I **Know** to Be True is ...."*

NOTICE the space that arises in which you can
choose to respond differently.
*"I feel empowered and supportive of
myself when I choose a new response."*

FEEL the relief.

Mindfulness

What I Know to Be True
is that in order to know what
is True for me, i need to first
detach from the emotion.

Powerful emotions can mask what I know at my core. Allowing the emotion to just be there, I can pause, take a breath, and discover that the emotion is not **who** I am, but simply a feeling.

Sitting with the feeling and moving through it will release its power.

Mindfulness

WHAT I KNOW TO BE TRUE
IS THAT IGNORING MY INNER GUIDANCE
CAUSES THE PROBLEM TO BECOME LARGER.

Tempting as it is to ignore my feelings,
or my body's negative manifestations
in the form of dis-ease, doing so will
only cause the problem to escalate.

I listen to my wise inner voice.

Mindfulness

WHAT I KNOW TO BE TRUE
IS THAT MY BODY IS A WISE
AND TRUSTED FRIEND.

My feelings and my body are constantly giving me messages to tell me when I am out of alignment with my inner self. The language of the body is sensation, not words.

I listen to the messages of my body...

Mindfulness

WHAT I KNOW TO BE TRUE

IS THAT BEING MINDFULLY PRESENT WITH MY

SUFFERING WILL HELP DISSOLVE THE PAIN.

Not being aware or present with pain and fear will cause me to run and struggle. Mindfulness simply means noticing what arises in the here and now. Gently attending to my wounded self in my suffering will help transform my pain.

Mindfulness

WHAT I KNOW TO BE TRUE
IS THAT A MINDFUL LIFE IS A MORE
PEACEFUL AND JOYFUL ONE.

Being mindful means being present and watching "what is." Noticing, without judgment. All it takes is practice.

Sit quietly and comfortably, bringing your attention to your breathing. Feel the sensation of the breath as it enters your body, in through your nose or mouth, down through your chest and into your belly. Bring full awareness to the feeling of the in-breath and the out-breath, in...out, in...out. If your mind wanders, as it will, just notice where it goes with idle curiosity and gently re-direct your attention back to your breath. Notice again the sensation of breathing in, and breathing out.

Breath in...breath out. There is nothing to be done right now, nowhere to go. Just be here now.

Emotions

What I Know to Be True
IS THAT I CAN LEARN TO SIT IN
UNCOMFORTABLE EMOTIONS KNOWING I AM
ABLE TO SOOTHE MY WAY THROUGH THEM.

When I am not centered, outside triggers will result in being hijacked by my own emotions, causing me to act out.

What I **Know** to Be True helps me to self-soothe and tolerate the strong emotions, trusting that I have the wisdom to keep myself safe from whatever comes my way.

Practice and compassion lessens the distress caused by heightened emotions and supports a return to a more balanced self.

Emotions

WHAT I KNOW TO BE TRUE
IS THAT I WILL BE HAPPIER WHEN I CAN
LEARN NOT TO TAKE THINGS PERSONALLY.

The degree to which I take things personally and react defensively is in direct correlation to the amount of hurt and fear I feel. I can begin to lower the walls of defensiveness that I have built over the years by learning to trust that I know what is True for me.

Emotions

WHAT I KNOW TO BE TRUE
IS THAT I CAN STAY TRUE TO MYSELF
WHEN I LEARN NOT TO TAKE ON THE
EMOTIONS & ENERGIES OF OTHERS.

When we stay connected to our core, we stay connected to that aspect of ourselves that is always love, compassion, safety and security. Our responsibility lies in protecting our energies, soothing our own sensitivities and staying in alignment with our own Truth, not trying to fix or take on the emotional energy of those around us.

Emotions

What I Know to Be True
IS THAT I AM BIGGER THAN MY EMOTIONS,
BIGGER THAN MY SITUATIONS.

Because I am in charge of myself, my actions
and my responses, I can rise above all that
otherwise threatens to pull me down.
Connecting with my Truth helps me adopt
a bird's eye view to provide a different
perspective. What once seemed so important
now appears much less significant.

Emotions

WHAT I KNOW TO BE TRUE
IS THAT LAUGHTER TRULY IS
THE BEST MEDICINE.

Life is joyful. Humor helps me detach from the "weight" of a situation, allowing me to gain perspective. Humor brings people together. Sharing a laugh lifts my physical vibration, strengthens the connection between myself & others and connects me with something greater than myself.

Practice shifting your mood by actively seeking something to laugh about.

Emotions

WHAT I KNOW TO BE TRUE
IS THAT TAKING THE RISK TO BE SEEN,
EVEN IN MY FAILURES OR MISTAKES,
HELPS ME BEGIN TO HEAL FROM SHAME.

Shame causes me to hide for fear of being judged; in my isolation I become both judge and jury. Only by shedding the cloak of shame am I able to embrace my self-worth and be free to create more authentic, meaningful relationships with myself and others.

Emotions

WHAT I KNOW TO BE TRUE
IS THAT FORGIVENESS OF MYSELF AND
OTHERS IS ESSENTIAL TO MY WELL BEING.

True healing comes only when I am
able to forgive myself and others
for the inevitable wounds that are
part of the human experience.

True forgiveness is not to condone, but to
accept and to release.
Judgment seals and shuts down.
Forgiveness heals and opens up.

Who do you need to forgive?
We invite you to start with yourself.

Emotions

IS THAT WHEN I AM FULLY ENGAGED, I

HAVE A MORE FULFILLING EXPERIENCE.

A partial commitment keeps me at arm's length from the experience and doesn't allow for full expression. Participating with total commitment brings greater satisfaction, the opportunity for real growth, and universal support.

Emotions

What I Know to Be True
is that my resistance has
a lot to teach me.

In order to let go of old patterns, it
is helpful to explore any resistance
and self-denial that may arise.

The resistance may be masking a fear
that hasn't yet been identified.

Don't be hard on yourself, just
notice, examine, and let go.

Emotions

WHAT I KNOW TO BE TRUE
IS THAT WHEN I BETTER UNDERSTAND
THE NATURE OF MY EMOTIONS, I AM ABLE
TO BE MORE IN CONTROL OF THEM.

Whereas external stimuli evoke an instinctive response, emotions are reactions to my mind's thoughts. When my thoughts are derived from habitual patterns, I simply need to notice the pattern and adjust the thought in order to shift the emotion.

Emotions

What I Know to Be True
is that I am my best self when
I balance heart and mind.

A wise soul will seek to find the
balance of both heart and mind.

Pause & reflect on your current
connection between heart and mind.
See it as an open corridor that links
the best of the wisdom from both.

*Use What I **Know** to Be True* to lead
with your heart intelligence.

Emotions

WHAT I KNOW TO BE TRUE
IS THAT WHEN I TUNE INTO MY
HEART, MY MIND CAN LET GO.

The mind does not have the desire to find peace and acceptance; the heart does.

Fear

WHAT I KNOW TO BE TRUE
IS THAT WHEN I FEEL SAFE AND SECURE, LIFE IS A GRAND ADVENTURE IN WHICH I AM EXCITED TO PLAY.

So many of my fears derive from believing I am not secure (in who I am, the decisions I make, my physical and financial well-being). Connecting with my higher Truth provides the security and foundation for a truly liberating life experience.

Fear

WHAT I KNOW TO BE TRUE
IS THAT I FEEL MORE EMPOWERED
WHEN I FACE MY FEARS.

Life can be challenging. Fear can paralyze me or make my wheels spin. Neither allows me to fully experience life. I have the capacity and the courage to be present in life, look directly at it, and experience it just the way it is, without being ruled by my fears.

"Whenever I meet my fears, I choose to turn towards love."

Fear

WHAT I KNOW TO BE TRUE
IS THAT I CAN CHOOSE NOT
TO HOOK INTO FEAR.

Living in a culture that thrives on fear makes it more imperative than ever not to feed the fear and allow it to disempower me. Adopting a stance of detachment to the emotion allows me to choose my response without getting hooked by the fear messages.

The result is a more peaceful and centered me, with the ability to rest quietly in the eye of the storm.

We invite you to write about your fears and ways in which you hook into them.

Fear

WHAT I KNOW TO BE TRUE
IS THAT I AM STRONG ENOUGH TO BE
VULNERABLE WITH MYSELF AND OTHERS.

Allowing myself to be vulnerable exhibits strength rather than weakness. Trusting myself to be vulnerable takes both courage and strength and allows me to truly be seen in the world. It is the foundation for intimate relationships and connection.

Fear

WHAT I KNOW TO BE TRUE
IS THAT WHEN I AM CONNECTED TO MY
ULTIMATE SOURCE OF SECURITY, I CAN
OPEN MY HEART WITHOUT FEAR.

Fear often makes me behave in ways
that are not a reflection of my best
self. Without worries or concerns I
am free to open my heart fully.

Perfection

WHAT I KNOW TO BE TRUE
IS THAT I AM PERFECT IN MY IMPERFECTION.

Looking in the mirror is hard because I have
to see my whole self, even the parts of me
that make me feel less worthy. Only when
I embrace and recognize the value of all
aspects of myself, will I be living in my Truth.

Perfection

What I Know to Be True
IS THAT THERE IS NO SUCH THING AS PERFECTION EXCEPT THAT WHICH IS FOUND IN IMPERFECTION.

Despite outside pressures that tell me to the contrary, there is no perfection. Looking to attain it guarantees certain failure and leaves me feeling less-than and worthless. Imagine a world where I can accept imperfection and **still** feel valuable and worthy!

Perfection

WHAT I KNOW TO BE TRUE
IS THAT I CAN SAFELY EMBRACE MY
WHOLE SELF, INCLUDING MY SHADOWS.

Who I am includes my shadow sides and those pieces of myself I don't care for. I have the courage to embrace them anyway, for the lessons they have to offer.

Self-Worth

WHAT I KNOW TO BE TRUE
IS THAT TO TRULY LOVE OTHERS,
I MUST FIRST LOVE MYSELF.

We all seem to have the same challenge, in
varying degrees: learning to love ourselves.

When I focus on all that is good, all
that I appreciate, and all that is unique
about myself, I can then send myself the
love I too often reserve for others.

"I deeply love and accept myself
just the way I am."

Self-Worth

What I Know to Be True
IS THAT IN ORDER TO EFFECTIVELY HELP
OTHERS, I NEED TO FIRST HEAL MYSELF.

My primary relationship is with myself.
Even though I can walk alongside another
to support their healing, I am ultimately
responsible only for my own healing.

Self-Worth

WHAT I KNOW TO BE TRUE
IS THAT WHEN I HONOR MY RELATIONSHIP
WITH MYSELF AS PRIMARY, I HAVE
HEALTHIER AND MORE MEANINGFUL
RELATIONSHIPS WITH OTHERS.

It is helpful to build a solid "vertical" relationship with myself by standing tall, closing my eyes and imagining that I have roots from the bottom of my feet deep into the earth, as well as a connection upwards from the crown of my head.

Try this exercise and feel how strong you are. It is from this place of vertical core strength that we can have healthy relationships with others.

Self-Worth

WHAT I KNOW TO BE TRUE
IS THAT SELF-CARE IS THE KEY
TO HEALTHY CARE-GIVING.

If my cup is empty I will not have enough
energy to give to myself or others the way
I would like. With my own cup full, I can
give without limit from the overflow.

Self-Worth

WHAT I KNOW TO BE TRUE
IS THAT MY SELF-WORTH IS NOT BASED
UPON WHAT OTHERS TELL ME.

I often determine my value based on external reflection, reinforcing myself as a victim of others and the outside world.

What I **Know** *to Be True* confirms and nourishes my inner power. It teaches me to embrace myself without requiring the approval, blessing or agreement of another.

Self-Worth

WHAT I KNOW TO BE TRUE
IS THAT MY TRUTH IS NOT FOUND BY
COMPARING MYSELF TO OR IMITATING OTHERS.

When I am not tuned into my own Truth, it is easy to copy or follow someone else. This will ultimately disconnect me further from my true Self.

When I connect with my own Truth I am free to be exactly who I really am. The more closely aligned I am with my Truth, the more authentic I am with myself and in my relationships with others.

Self-Worth

What I Know to Be True
is that it is none of my business
what others think of me.

⸻ ⸻

I cannot control what others think or
believe. All I can do is be True to myself and
everything will unfold in perfect order.

Self-Worth

WHAT I KNOW TO BE TRUE
IS THAT I AM NOT THE STORIES I
TELL ABOUT MYSELF.

How often does the drama of the day or week becomes the topic of conversation, falsely defining who I am? But I am not my stories. Only by letting go of the drama am I able to share who I really am.

Notice the story you are telling daily, weekly. Notice how you may use that story to anchor you in the moment.

Notice how many people you share your story with each day, each week. What happens if you stop telling the story and disengage from the drama?

Self-Worth

WHAT I KNOW TO BE TRUE
IS THAT REALIZING MY TRUE VALUE HELPS
ME MAKE POSITIVE, CONSTRUCTIVE CHOICES.

Feeling unworthy causes me to make choices
that support my sense of unworthiness
and keep me in an unhealthy cycle. Tapping
into my Truth allows me to actualize
my self-worth, reversing the spiral.

Judgment

WHAT I KNOW TO BE TRUE
IS THAT I ALLOW OTHERS TO BE THEIR TRUE
SELVES WHEN I DO NOT JUDGE THEM.

The acceptance of my fellow humans without judgment is a gift beyond measure. And what a gift in return, should they bestow the same acceptance upon me.

Judgment

WHAT I KNOW TO BE TRUE
IS THAT I CAN RELEASE ALL JUDGMENT
OF MYSELF AND OTHERS.

⁓

There is no benefit to judgment except to further separate us from our true nature.

"I accept and love myself just the way I am. I accept and love others just as they are."

Judgment

WHAT I KNOW TO BE TRUE
IS THAT WHEN I FOCUS ON THE BEST
ASPECTS OF ANOTHER PERSON, THOSE
ARE THE QUALITIES THAT WILL BE
AMPLIFIED AND REFLECTED.

Continuously using a viewfinder that highlights the differences or things that bother me about others creates separation and judgment. Shifting my visual lens to accentuate the best and brightest about others creates an environment in which we will both flourish.

Judgment

WHAT I KNOW TO BE TRUE
IS THAT MY RELATIONSHIP WITH OTHERS
WILL FLOURISH WHEN I DON'T MAKE
ASSUMPTIONS OR JUMP TO CONCLUSIONS.

Wrongly drawn conclusions, often based on erroneous perception, cause needless pain and suffering in my relationships. When I take the risk to really see and hear others, my relationships become more meaningful.

Practice listening...to yourself
and those you love.

Responsibility

WHAT I KNOW TO BE TRUE
IS THAT TAKING RESPONSIBILITY FOR MY
ACTIONS AND MY RESPONSES IS LIBERATING.

Blaming others makes me feel
powerless and puts me in a victim
role, leading to further distress.

Taking responsibility releases the connection
that binds me to those I blame, thereby
freeing me into a more open, healing state.

Responsibility

WHAT I KNOW TO BE TRUE
IS THAT I, AND I ALONE, AM RESPONSIBLE
FOR MY CHOICES AND DECISIONS.

When I make choices and decisions
founded in love, gratitude and acceptance,
rather than from fear, lack or blame, I
am truly in charge of my well-being.

LISA JACOBY & CAROLINE J TEMPLE

Validation

WHAT I KNOW TO BE TRUE
IS THAT NO EXTERNAL VALIDATION
IS REQUIRED WHEN I AM STANDING
IN MY OWN TRUTH.

When I find myself looking to others for validation, it is time to pause and look within. Is it true for **me**? That is enough.

When I am standing in my own Truth I have the self-confidence and courage to know that what I say, feel and do are in alignment.

Validation

WHAT I KNOW TO BE TRUE
IS THAT WHEN I AM TAPPED INTO MY
TRUTH I NO LONGER NEED TO JUSTIFY,
RATIONALIZE OR EXPLAIN MYSELF.

So often I feel the need to provide
a reason for what I do by offering a
rationalization or justification.

When I stop judging myself and my behavior,
and stop worrying about what others
think of me, I can embrace my actions
without the need for explanation.

Validation

WHAT I KNOW TO BE TRUE
IS THAT SOMETIMES WHEN I SPEAK
MY OWN TRUTH, IT MAY BE HARD
FOR OTHERS TO HEAR IT.

Others may invalidate, object to, deny or simply not be able to hear my Truth. That may indeed be the case. That person's response is not my responsibility or within my control.

My responsibility lies only in Knowing and acknowledging my own Truth.

Validation

WHAT I KNOW TO BE TRUE
IS THAT WHEN I REALLY START
HEARING MY OWN TRUTH, I WON'T
NEED TO LEARN IT FROM OTHERS.

So often I use the words of others,
especially well-known authors or
influential spiritual teachers, to support
my own Truth. That is all good.

However, when I am truly tapped
into my own Truth and knowing, and
can accept myself fully, I can let go of
the need for constant validation.

Validation

WHAT I KNOW TO BE TRUE
IS THAT I WILL BE HAPPIER WHEN
I FOLLOW MY OWN HEART RATHER
THAN TAKE ACTION BASED UPON THE
BELIEFS OR REACTIONS OF OTHERS.

When I connect with Source, my very own Truth, I am in alignment with who I really am. I then come from a place of strength and knowing, without being affected by external influences.

Control

WHAT I KNOW TO BE TRUE
IS THAT I CAN LET GO OF MY
WORRIES BECAUSE THINGS WILL
LOOK DIFFERENTLY TOMORROW.

When anxiety arises, I can find peace of mind knowing that tomorrow holds possibility that eludes me today, even if I can't yet see it or don't know what shape it will take. Each moment is but a fleeting one.

Control

WHAT I KNOW TO BE TRUE
IS THAT I CAN RELINQUISH CONTROL BY
ALLOWING EVENTS TO UNFOLD NATURALLY.

Rather than trying to control the world around me, I can choose to release my attachment to the outcome and the anxiety that comes with trying to force my will on circumstances beyond my control. Learning to trust the universe is powerful and allows life to unfold in perfect order.

Control

WHAT I KNOW TO BE TRUE
IS THAT WHEN I STOP TRYING TO
CONTROL SOMEONE ELSE'S BEHAVIOR, I
AM MORE ATTENTIVE TO MY OWN.

Whenever I find myself wanting to control another's behavior, I know that it is based upon my own needs and insecurities.

Pause and ask yourself: where is this desire for control coming from?

Control

What I Know to Be True
IS THAT I FEEL MORE IN CONTROL WHEN I
STOP TRYING TO CONTROL THE SITUATION
AND SIMPLY CHANGE MY RESPONSE.

Paradoxically, the myth is that I am in control at all. In reality, when I embrace my lack of control, I am able to live with greater ease. Think of a situation that is upsetting you and try changing your response to it using *What I* **Know** *to Be True*. How does it feel different?

Ask yourself about your need to control. Watch what happens when you let go...

Control

WHAT I KNOW TO BE TRUE
IS THAT WHEN I LET GO OF TRYING TO
FIX THINGS OVER WHICH I HAVE NO
CONTROL, I CONSERVE ENERGY AND
ACTUALLY FEEL MORE IN CONTROL.

Holding on to the desire to fix
something or someone is like taking an
uncomfortable journey to nowhere.

Let go of the reins.

Trust

WHAT I KNOW TO BE TRUE
IS THAT MY LIFE FLOWS WITH GRACE
AND EASE WHEN I LEARN TO TRUST
MYSELF AND FOLLOW MY OWN TRUTH.

The journey to a more joyful, peaceful life often involves walking through the darkness of painful experiences and feelings. Regular use of the practice of *What I* **Know** *to Be True* helps me trust my own Knowing to provide safe passage.

Trust

WHAT I KNOW TO BE TRUE
IS THAT IF I TAKE THE RISK TO TRUST
IN MY TRUTH, I WILL LIVE A RICHER,
FULLER AND MORE REWARDING LIFE.

The more I take the risk to trust that I
know what is best for me, the greater
trust resources I will have to draw on
the next time the doubt returns.

Trust

WHAT I KNOW TO BE TRUE
IS THAT I TRUST IN SOMETHING BIGGER
THAN MYSELF AND AM THEN ABLE
TO HOLD THE VISION I CREATE.

When I tap into my own Truth, I can more easily trust that everything is unfolding the way it is meant to and the universe will support me in realizing my dreams.

"I trust in my abilities and set my intentions."

Trust

WHAT I KNOW TO BE TRUE
IS THAT ALL IS WELL.

When I let go of my attachment to the outcome and stop projecting my own need for control, I gain a greater sense of trust that all is indeed well with my world.

Change

WHAT I KNOW TO BE TRUE
IS THAT CHANGE IS CONSTANT.

When I embrace change as inevitable, rather than resist it, each and every moment delivers greater fulfillment, and fear is greatly reduced.

Change

WHAT I KNOW TO BE TRUE
IS THAT I CAN MANIFEST THE
CHANGE THAT I SEEK.

Change begins when I stop giving energy and nourishment to negative thoughts and feelings. I can simply rest peacefully in my inner stillness and focus on my desired vision.

Connection

WHAT I KNOW TO BE TRUE
IS THAT WHEN I GENUINELY AND OPENLY
CONNECT WITH OTHERS, I FEEL MORE AT
EASE WITH MYSELF, OTHERS, AND THE
UNIVERSAL ENERGY ALL AROUND ME.

We all have a fundamental need for connection with others. If I believe I am separate, I open the door to loneliness, isolation and depression. If I focus on feeling connected, I will be uplifted and energized.

Connection

WHAT I KNOW TO BE TRUE
IS THAT WE ARE ALL CONNECTED.

When I tap into the Source energy that is the universe, I understand that all is one, that I am connected to all others, and to all living energy. This perspective helps to change my relationship with others and with the world at large.

Think about it...
Know it...

Connection

WHAT I KNOW TO BE TRUE
IS THAT LOVING OURSELVES OPENS
THE DOOR TO LOVING HUMANITY.

I am taught to love my neighbor, but without
loving myself first, I often fall short.
Nourishment of the individual leads
to nourishment of the collective.

Expansion

WHAT I KNOW TO BE TRUE
IS THAT CONTRACTION IS THE
PAUSE BEFORE EXPANSION.

Contraction is often viewed as a negative
state, whereas in reality, it is simply the
converse of expansion. Just as with breathing,
contraction is required for expansion to occur.

I can inwardly contract by quietly
reconnecting with myself in order
to effectively expand and grow.

Expansion

What I Know to Be True
IS THAT HOLDING A SENSE OF
SPACIOUSNESS ALLOWS ME TO SUSTAIN
ALL THAT LIFE OFFERS ME.

When I hold the space for all that life offers me, both painful and joyous, I feel the ultimate support of being present to myself as a friend. It becomes the support on which I can always count.

Expansion

What I Know to Be True
is that when i connect with my
own Truth, i live in a more open,
expanded, spacious state.

Expansion connects me with
my personal power.

We invite you to close your eyes whileopening
your arms wide, feeling the expansion of
your chest and the opening of your heart.

Take a few deep cleansing breaths
and notice how you feel.

After a few moments, contract your body;
make yourself small by wrapping your arms
around yourself and crossing your legs.

Feel the difference between the two states.

Expansion

What I Know to Be True

IS THAT I AM FILLED WITH HOPE AND
POSSIBILITY WHEN I AM IN AN
EXPANDED STATE.

※

Expansion opens me up to explore. Without
limitations anything is possible and I can
be excited about what lies ahead.

Appreciation

WHAT I KNOW TO BE TRUE
IS THAT I FEEL BETTER WHEN
I TREAT MYSELF AND OTHERS
WITH LOVING KINDNESS.

The energy I express is reflected back to me.

Appreciation

WHAT I KNOW TO BE TRUE
IS THAT I INVITE ABUNDANCE
WHEN I EMBRACE AN ATTITUDE OF
APPRECIATION AND GRATITUDE.

Focusing on what I appreciate shifts
my thoughts away from my perception
of "not enough" to one of believing
that my needs will be met.

We invite you to start a gratitude practice
morning and night. Note what it is that
you are grateful for as you wake up
and as you close your eyes to sleep.

Appreciation

WHAT I KNOW TO BE TRUE
IS THAT WHEN I AM APPRECIATIVE
OF WHO I AM AND WHAT I HAVE,
MY LIFE IS MORE MEANINGFUL.

Getting caught up in the search for more, constantly seeking what I don't have, causes increased self-absorption and fantasy thinking, such as "I'll be happy when…"

Recognizing how blessed I am in each moment creates room for expansion on every level.

Giving/Receiving

WHAT I KNOW TO BE TRUE
IS THAT I AM IN BALANCE WHEN
I BOTH GIVE *AND* RECEIVE.

I often find it easier to give than to receive,
which leads to a feeling of depletion. When
I try to give from an empty vessel, I signal
the universe that I come from lack.

As a full vessel, I give freely from strength and
love rather than from need or expectation.

Receiving acknowledges my worthiness and
my inherent desire for abundance. By learning
to receive, I acknowledge my worthiness.

Giving/Receiving

What I Know to Be True
IS THAT A TRUE GIFT FROM THE HEART
IS OFFERED WITH NO EXPECTATIONS.

When I give with the expectation of reward, payback or gold star, I am giving with strings attached.

Unconditional giving recognizes that the reward is an energetic one and cannot readily be defined.

Contrast

WHAT I KNOW TO BE TRUE
IS THAT WITHOUT CONTRAST IN MY LIFE,
I WOULD NOT FULLY APPRECIATE THE
EXTRAORDINARY NATURE OF BEING ALIVE.

I need darkness in order to know light,
cold in order to feel warmth, chaos to
recognize order, conflict to experience
peace. I embrace it all, for the contrast
is essential to my experience.

Meaning and Purpose

WHAT I KNOW TO BE TRUE
IS THAT IT'S A MIRACLE JUST TO BE ALIVE.

"I am grateful for the gift of each in-breath and each out-breath that reminds me that I am alive."

Meaning and Purpose

WHAT I KNOW TO BE TRUE
IS THAT I HAVE VALUE SIMPLY
BECAUSE I AM ALIVE.

My self-worth has nothing to do with my actions, possessions or relationships. By virtue of the fact that I am a human being, I have value that is immeasurable.

Meaning and Purpose

WHAT I KNOW TO BE TRUE
IS THAT CONNECTING WITH MY TRUTH HELPS
ME FIND MEANING AND PURPOSE IN MY LIFE.

Now more than ever, I need to connect
with my own Truth in order to connect
with the magnificence of life on this planet
and with my fellow human beings.

I find peace when I take full responsibility for
my own alignment–with integrity and truth in
my actions, my relationships, my community,
my planet, the world at large, and the universe.

Balance

WHAT I KNOW TO BE TRUE
IS THAT WHEN I AM CONNECTED TO MY
TRUTH, MY LIFE FEELS MORE IN BALANCE.

It is not possible to stay in balance all the time. It requires constant vigilance and readjustment. When I strive for alignment between what I feel, think, say and do, I find a more peaceful and centered place within, one that is fully supported by the universe.

Take a snapshot of where you are today. Look at balance and imbalance in your life.

What do you notice?

Harmony

WHAT I KNOW TO BE TRUE
IS THAT PURE JOY AND CLARITY EMERGE
WHEN I EMBRACE AND HARMONIZE THE
SEPARATE AND DIVERSE ASPECTS OF MY LIFE.

My life experiences, while often seemingly
discordant, comprise the rich medley
of my own internal orchestra. When I
live in Truth, each individual experience
operates in harmony with the other,
creating an undeniable symphony.

Walk the Talk

WHAT I KNOW TO BE TRUE
IS THAT MY DAILY CHALLENGE IS TO
WALK THE WALK AND TALK THE TALK.

How can I set my intention to do
just that today and everyday?

What I Know to Be True

WHAT I KNOW TO BE TRUE
IS THAT WHAT I SEEK I ALREADY KNOW.

When I tap into my core, my Knowingness,
my own Truth, I know exactly what
is right for me in every situation.

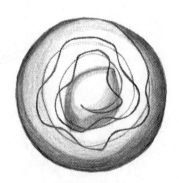

Remember Who
You Really Are

At a time when the world is crying out for change, it's up to each of us to fuel that change. Lasting change can only be created from the inside out, beginning with each individual and trusting that such a shift in each one of us has the power to cause a ripple effect greater than we can imagine. We are being asked to look within, find our higher Truth, embrace our gifts and use them for the greater good. This is only truly possible when we know who we really are and are fully connected to our Truth.

In order to know who we really are and create a new reality, we must change our relationship with our emotions, our thoughts, and ultimately with our ego selves. You can follow the path to remember who you are on an on-going basis through the practice of *What I* **Know** *to Be True*.

In discovering your own Truth, your life will change. You may be letting go of who you thought you were. Or it may not be such a dramatic change. But either way, *once you've been there and experienced the peace, you'll want to return as often as possible.*

Allow others to use *What I* **Know** *to Be True* to tap into their own inner core, in their own way. How they use it is entirely up to them; each of us can only be responsible for our own empowerment. Practicing this will spill over into all aspects of your life. *Allow* *others to live their lives without your judgment and you will start doing the same for yourself.*

*What I **Know** to Be True* will help you live the more centered, peaceful and conscious life you seek. There is no need for judgment or drama, for it is simply a *return* path to a self that you have forgotten. It will help you remember your *own* Truth, not someone else's truth for you. It will help you to remember that **what you seek you already know.**

If at any time you find you want your life to be easier, step back into *What You **Know** to Be True.* When drama creeps into your relationships, *What I **Know** to Be True* will help you to respond with grace and ease. When you need to free yourself from the addiction to the anticipatory rush of emotional energy and pain that comes from trying to be in control of everything and everyone, *What I **Know** to Be True* will be your friend. When you are ready to reveal more of yourself to the world in Truth, *What I **Know** to Be True* will help you do just that. When you want to *feel* and honor your own Truth, not someone else's truth for you, *What I **Know** to Be True* will help you guide yourself down that path. When you are ready to change your life, *What I **Know** to Be True* will help you make lasting changes from the inside out.

When you remember who you really are, you will also remember the pure guidance you have within you. Remember to explore your own *Truth* through *feeling.* Get comfortable *feeling* your own *Truth.* Express your own *Truth* out loud. Capture your own *Truth* in writing. Decide to live your own *Truth* and allow others to live theirs. Live your life in the only way that truly matters, from your own *Truth.*

*Feel, honor and express your
Truth each and every day.*

*What we Know to Be True is that
this is all that really matters.*

*You are the Gateway,
What I **Know** to Be True is the Key.*

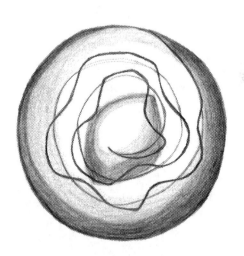

We invite you to visit our website, WhatIKnowtoBeTrue.com to learn more about our work, find out about upcoming events, and to receive a free audio meditation.

With love and appreciation,
~Lisa & Caroline~

About the Authors

Lisa Jacoby:

After an executive career with Fortune 500 companies and as an entrepreneur, Lisa now uses her skills to assist businesses tap into their core and become the best they can be. A lifetime's curiosity and spiritual exploration helped her develop and lead support and resource groups focused on holistic health and spiritual growth. In addition, Lisa published Natural Awakenings, a community mind/body/spirit magazine. She continues to pursue her passion for connecting people with community and lives in Connecticut with her husband and two children.
YourInterimCOO.com
WhatIKnowtoBeTrue.com

Caroline J. Temple:

Originally from England, Caroline is a holistic psychotherapist incorporating traditional and spiritual approaches, Reiki and life coaching, in her private therapy practice. After an early career in advertising, followed by several years raising her three children, Caroline earned her MSW in order to pursue a passion for working with women in a therapeutic setting. Through counseling she seeks to empower and support her clients on their respective inner and outer journeys. She continues to actively explore her own personal and spiritual growth.
MyWiseWoman.com
WhatIKnowtoBeTrue.com

Anna Linley, Icon Artist:

Anna is an Intuitive Artist and Energy Healing Practitioner. For six years she used art as a healing modality for herself. Art permitted Anna to explore her inner self by allowing images to find their way into her painting. In turn, these explorations helped Anna develop her gifts as an intuitive artist and healer. TulkuHealing.com